I, Truther

My 9/11 Truth Quest

and subsequent truth-seeking activities

David F. Palmer

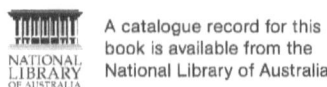
A catalogue record for this book is available from the National Library of Australia

Copyright © 2023 David Frank Palmer
All Rights Reserved
ISBN-13: 978-1-922727-84-8

Proudly printed in Australia
First published by
Linellen Press
265 Boomerang Road
Oldbury, Western Australia
www.linellenpress.com.au

Contents

Executive Summary 1
Life before my 9/11 Truth Quest 4
Initial Suspicions about 9/11 8
My first US 9/11 related trip 14
Getting serious about 9/11 Truth 17
My advices to the Australian Federal Police 19
Taking a different approach to 9/11 Truth 23
My second US 9/11 related trip 28
Joining the 9/11 Truth network 30
The Foreign Influence Transparency Scheme 33
The Outcome of the US Court Cases 43
My 9/11 Truth Quest continues 45
My Royal Commission submission 47
Western Australia 52
Conclusions about 9/11 Truth in Australia 64
Where to from here? 68
My thoughts on the COVID-19 outbreak 72
My thoughts on the AUKUS security pact 80
Wrapping Up 86
Appendix 1 – My Draft Master's Thesis 90
Appendix 2 - Who Governs America? 121
Appendix 3 – 9/11 Research Report 123
Appendix 4 – 9/11 Report Addendum 135
Appendix 5 - Updated Summary of my 9/11 Research 138

Appendix 6 - My attempts to speak Truth to Power in Australia with respect to the 9/11 Event 152
Appendix 7 – The Global Financial Elite 168
Appendix 8 – Royal Commission's replies in full 195
Appendix 9 - My AUKUS Submission 200
About the Author 206

Executive Summary

The purpose of the book is to provide a start-to-finish account of my 9/11 advocacy from an early interest in American Foreign Policy to my final conclusion of the futility of trying to get the Australian Government to acknowledge that they already know all that I have reported over the past 20 years.

Much of the narrative has already been published either as appendices in my novel *Amerissance* or in the Research reports section of my book *Wondering*.

A succinct summary of the key pieces of evidence that prove that the official 9/11 narrative is false includes:

1. The laws of physics say that the twin towers of the World Trade Center could not have collapsed all the way to the ground due to gravity alone.

2. According to Prof Leroy Hulsey, WTC7 could not have collapsed in the way that the National Institute of Standards and Technology (NIST) said it did. Hulsey's report is currently being scientifically reviewed by a Technical Advisory Committee within the UK's Institution of Mechanical Engineers. The review will also look at other explanations for the collapse.

3. More than 150 eye-witnesses heard explosions before and during the collapse of all three WTC buildings.

4. Traces of explosives/incendiary residues were found in

the dust of Lower Manhattan after 9/11.

5. Seismic recordings of the collapses support controlled demolition, not gravity collapse.

6. Islamic extremists could not have directed the movements of the US Air Force on 9/11.

7. NIST's and Bažant's accounts of the three WTC building collapses have been persuasively debunked by impressive scholarship by many competent researchers and dedicated activists.

8. Bush said, at his first cabinet meeting, "find me a way to do this", meaning invade Iraq.

9. Prior to 9/11, the Project for the New American Century called for a "New Pearl Harbour".

10. The majority of American respondents to 9/11 Truth Action Project's survey said that it was reasonable to suspect the US Government's account on 9/11.

My communications with leading politicians, senior bureaucrats, the media, and specific entities, like the Foreign Influence Transparency Scheme, the Royal Commission into Defence and Veterans Suicide and the Returned and Services League of Australia, all demonstrate that no one in the Australian Government or any other influential organization is going to contradict the US Government on its 9/11 narrative. That is particularly so in light of the new Australia United Kingdom United States (AUKUS) security agreement and Australia's continued and enhanced integration of the Australian Defence Force into the American command structure. The

Strategic Defence Review 2023 confirms such enhanced interoperability. It also effectively concludes that Australia cannot defend itself against an adversary the size of China and needs a great power ally to do so.

Speculation that the COVID-19 event is related to 9/11 is reasonable when consideration is given to the long line of lies and deception for which the US Government is well known; from the two Kennedy and Martin Luther King assassinations to the Gulf of Tonkin incident, to the lies about the US ability to win the Vietnam War, to the lies about Saddam Hussein's weapons of mass destruction, and now the proven knowledge that the US was doing "gain-of-function" research on bat-borne corona viruses before 2014, when Obama banned it in the US; that US scientists then outsourced it to Wuhan to continue the research; but then Trump lifted the ban. The extent of the private sector-driven contract "gain-of-function" research (138 separate contracts according to one source) was reported at some length at the Stockholm conference referred to in Appendix 7.

The latest Australian defence policy and strategy demonstrate that Australia is no longer an independent sovereign nation, if it ever was. It is a vassal state of the American Empire. My submission to the Australian Government, reported in Appendix 9, protests this fact.

Life before my 9/11 Truth Quest

This is a true story. I know it's a true story because it's about me. I lived it. I know its only character – me – as well as I know myself; for I am he. I will not tell you all of my story, because it would bore you, most of it anyway, for I am a simple man, a man of no great talent or accomplishment, just an ordinary man like your dad, your uncle, your neighbor, or, to take that acquaint old English legal phrase, "the man of the Clapham omnibus".

This story covers that period of my life from 2002 to 2023 inclusive, spanning my fifty-fourth to my seventy-fifth years of age. It does not cover a triumphant part of my life, more a time of effort, disappointment, frustration and, occasionally, despair, but not an uneventful period. It has kept me busy. It has given me a reason to get out of bed in the morning, even at times at 2.30 am and 3.30 am in the morning. It still does, for I am not done yet, not if I can help it.

A brief biography of me is contained at the end of this book.

So, without further ado, here is my story. I pick up this partial autobiography in 2002.

In that and the subsequent year, my twenty-year career as a management consultant came to an end. It was partly my fault, inasmuch as, in that year, I terminated a rather successful and lucrative collaboration with a professional colleague. We were not legally partners, but did work closely together and had been successful in penetrating the consulting market for business planning services to four different Western Australian universities, each of whom needed professionally prepared business plans to support their various grant applications for research funding.

The first of these successful opportunities came via an invitation to my associate, even though I actually wrote the proposal that won the work, so all subsequent invitations were also directed to him with me being engaged as his associate. When I terminated the association, due to personality clashes, those opportunities continued to go to him and I was excluded from further involvement in that business stream.

So successful had been our collaboration, in fact, that it had consumed almost all of my time over the preceding five years, so its loss to me left me with little follow-on income. That meant I had to restart my consulting career all over just like a "newbie" to the profession. It sounded a bit daunting but I was confident at the time that my reputation as a competent professional in my field of expertise would ensure my successful regeneration.

Unfortunately, events beyond my control conspired to frustrate my efforts to re-establish myself. 2003 proved to be a very difficult year economically for the whole of Western Australia. Then there was a change in the State Government from a Liberal to Labor party administration. Changes of government were always bad for the consulting profession because incoming governments tended to regard consultants as merely being political cronies of the previous regime. They tended to shun them completely; until they subsequently discovered that they actually needed the expertise that specialist professionals could provide, so slowly the work came back. I was state president of the Institute of Management Consultants at the time and it fell to me to open up a new dialogue with the incoming regime on behalf of the entire profession to assist that regeneration.

A further challenge came from a policy of the incoming government to "get the dead wood out of the public service".

This policy resulted in several senior public servants – particularly those aged over fifty-five years of age, a number of whom I knew personally – having their futures "freed up". I was not a public servant, but the idea of getting rid of anyone over fifty-five, a classic case of age discrimination even if it was official government policy, pervaded not only within the public service but extended to all those businesses that contracted to the government. I was only fifty-four at the time, but I looked older, so that discrimination extended to me. Work from the public sector in the 2002/03 year practically dried up as a result.

I had three children at university at the time, and I was keen not to disrupt their studies, so my wife and I struggled on without bringing our financial situation to their attention. We survived on our savings, and when they ran out, by running up my credit cards to their maximum. My main objective at that time was to just hang on long enough for each of them to graduate.

We succeeded, almost, but by the end of June 2003 my credit cards were almost "maxed out" and I was left with only a modest income from part-time teaching and a few small consulting assignments. It was not enough. Something else had to give.

The only other financial resource that we had available to us was the modest amount that I had built up in my private superannuation accounts. But that was only available at age fifty-five and only if I formally retired. That provided our only viable opportunity to carry on.

So, on 30th June 2003, two days after my fifty-fifth birthday, I formally retired. That allowed me to access my modest superannuation savings and provided sufficient funds for the family to carry on till the end of the year.

But by January 2004, even that resource had been exhausted, and two of the kids had yet to graduate. So, we went back into drawing on credit card funding. That took us through to June

2004. Then those credit cards were again "maxed out".

My wife is a very astute woman when it comes to money. She saw the writing on the wall long before I did.

"We are going to have to sell the house," she said.

"No, no," I protested. "I'll pull a rabbit out of the hat. Trust me, you'll see."

My wife is a much more realistic person than me. I'm somewhat of a dreamer, an idealist, an optimist, always hoping, and expecting that something would come along to rescue us. And so it did, eventually: my father died and left me a small legacy, enough to be going on with. Then my mother-in-law decided that it was time to claim her heavenly reward. Since my wife was an only child, she inherited the whole of her mother's estate. We've been comfortably well off ever since.

But the rescue came about a year too late. By the end of May 2005, we put the house on the market. It sold within three weeks. That's what kept the bailiff at bay. But it forced the kids to leave home and go out into the world to make their own way, and it forced my wife and me to seek a more modest abode in a less prestigious neighbourhood.

The failure practically broke me spiritually. When I first announced to my wife back in 1982 that I was not going to look for another job but was going to start my own business, she said: "That's fine by me. Just promise me that you will never put my home at risk." I promptly did so. Twenty years later I broke that promise. About that time, I practically gave up on life. I just didn't care anymore. I don't deal well with failure.

Initial Suspicions about 9/11

Not all was lost, however. I still had a couple of small part-time teaching assignments, one at post-graduate level and another at undergraduate level. I had also embarked upon an academic program at the Australian National University leading to a graduate diploma in Security Studies, a field in which I had long been interested. The program included units in Military Strategy and Military Planning as well as Strategic Geography and Military Security Complexes like the security situation in the Indian Ocean and Persian Gulf theatre, a focus that was most appropriate for a West Australian.

Unfortunately, a series of administrative "foul-ups" placed my continued participation in that ANU program in jeopardy and I transferred to a complementary program majoring in International Relations (IR) at a local university. My academic record proved useful there because I already had a Master's Degree from that university and was granted advanced standing to its IR program.

In June 2004, I completed and was awarded a Graduate Diploma in International Relations from Curtin University of Technology. I immediately enrolled in a Master's program in the same discipline. I got as far as completing the first draft of a 10,000-word thesis, which I submitted to my superior for evaluation. He scribbled red ink comments all over it and handed it back to me, commenting that he thought I was talking nonsense, and instructed me to go back and start again. I was quite shocked at his assessment. I anticipated that he would criticize it, that's why post-graduate students have supervisors, but I wasn't expecting such a scathing assessment.

Needless to say, I didn't think that my draft deserved such treatment. I did not think that my assessment of the contemporary situation in International Relations was so wrong that it warranted such severe criticism. So, I withdrew from that Master's program.

About a year later, my supervisor's own book was published. I bought a copy and read it. To my surprise I found that my thesis had directly contradicted his own assessment, and his own predictions, for the future of Australia's military alliance with the United States, the ANZUS treaty (Australia, New Zealand and United States). Interestingly, a few years later, I met up with him again and he commented: "Just because I disagree with you does not mean that you are wrong."

Another interesting development on the same theme occurred around the same time. I was at a conference on national security in Fremantle and had the opportunity to talk with the immediate past United States Consul-General to Western Australia. She was married to an Australian and had stayed on in Perth on the completion of her two-year tour of duty with the State Department in W.A. So, I told her about my draft Master's thesis and its main conclusion, namely, that I expected the United States would withdraw its military forces back from west of Guam by 2025. My main reasoning was that I thought US debt levels were getting so high America would not be able to maintain its global dominance for more than another two decades. She just looked me straight in the eye and said quite bluntly, "By 2020."

This was before the 2008-09 Global Financial Crisis and before the Trump presidency. So clearly, someone in the US State Department must have also been thinking: "We just can't keep this up." And my insights into the growing tensions within

American society about the growing cost of maintaining the American Empire also seemed to fairly be well-founded.

So you can judge the soundness of my reasoning, my January 2005 draft Master's thesis is reproduced in Appendix 1 to this work. It was written in the third person at the time. This is the first time this narrative has been published.

My draft Master's thesis was the global geopolitical situation as I perceived it in January 2005. Most of the statistics reported therein are, of course, out of date. But many, if not most, of the essential themes contained within my 2005 thesis are, I believe, still valid nearly twenty years later. My timing is probably out by a few years, but contemporary American foreign policy does seem to avoid direct military interventions in foreign wars but to sponsor local belligerents to conduct proxy wars, with their people doing the fighting and the United States providing the arms, supplies and ordinance, with, of course, American industry reaping the financial rewards of these endeavours, even if American taxpayers are doing most of the paying. The current war in Ukraine appears to feature this kind of arrangement and, if war does break out over Taiwan, then I suspect it will be the Taiwanese people who will be doing most of the fighting and dying.

But, in 2005, even though I had formally withdrawn from my academic research program, I, nevertheless, continued my research into contemporary International Relations in a private capacity. Since I had formally retired from the workforce, I had plenty of time on my hands even though I was still doing some part-time teaching at two Western Australian universities. Moreover, those last-mentioned activities gave me access to the full spectrum of university research facilities which I considered to be a very valuable resource.

In July 2005, I purchased a book from Amazon.com entitled

Crossing the Rubicon by Michael C. Rupert[1]. In it, Rupert, a former Los Angeles Police Department narcotics investigator, expressed the view that if he had been in charge of the investigation into the mass murders that took place in New York City and Washington D.C. on 11th September 2001 (commonly known as 9/11) he believed that he had sufficient evidence to lay criminal charges against the senior members of the Bush Administration for the crime of mass murder. To my mind, it is an astonishing book. But having read it, I said to myself: "Boy, that's an amazing story." Then I quietly filed it on the bookshelf in my study and proceeded to reach for the next book on my reading list.

With plenty of time on my hands and little interest in the usual retirement activities such as golf, lawn bowls, fishing and so on – the types of pastimes that most mature-aged Australian males fill up their retirement with – I thought I would try my hand at writing. I had written many things throughout my career, but most of them were reports of one kind or another, and, of course, plenty of academic papers. Now it was "me time" so I thought I would just write for my own satisfaction.

My first novel was entitled "*Armaginning: Armageddon New Beginning*" which I published in 2009. I wrote it mainly to see if I could. It was an interesting learning experience. It took me a whole year to write and another year to edit and proofread, with eight edits, no less. I'm not sure whether that is normal or not but that's what it took me.

Its main theme was to explore the question of who really runs the world. Who is the Global Elite, so to speak? I thought then, and still do now, that there must be a small group of individuals who orchestrate the major geopolitical events of the world, or the Western World at least, if not the communist world, China

---

[1] (New Society Publishers, Grabriola Island, BC, Canada, 2004)

in particular, and the Russian Federation.

The key antagonist in this initial story I called the "Global Strategy Council" (GSC for short) and the hero was a fictional American retired military officer who was modelled on an Australian brigadier I had met a few years earlier on a trip to Egypt, as were many of the supporting characters in the story.

During the late first decade of the 21st century, years, my wife and I also managed to indulge in a little overseas travel like the above-mentioned trip to Egypt. We had not done any travel since the late 1970s, during which time we had visited twenty-eight countries, most of which were included in an overland road trip from London to Katmandu on the back of a truck. In our later years, we had definitely graduated to the five-star international hotel and guided tour type of travel. We also managed to fit in New Zealand and a couple of trips to the eastern states to visit one of our daughters who had moved to Melbourne.

A few years later, in late 2009, I came across an academic paper entitled: *Active Themitic Material Discovered in Dust from the 9/11 World Trade Centre Catastrophe*[2]. I noted that one of the authors of the paper, Frank Legge, had recorded a business address in Subiaco, a suburb in the Western Australian capital city of Perth. So, I looked up Dr Legge in the local trade directory and called him up on the telephone.

I said to Frank: "Look, I'm not a technical person so please tell me if I'm reading your paper correctly. Are you telling me that the Twin Towers of the World Trade Center were brought down by a controlled demolition?"

---

[2] Harrit, Niels H., Farrer, Jeffrey, Jones, Steven E., Ryan, Kevin R., Legge, Frank M., Farnsworth, Daniel, Roberts, Greg, Gourley, James R. and Larsen, Bradley R., *Active Themitic Material Discovered in Dust from the 9/11 World Trade Centre Catastrophe*, The Open Chemical Physics Journal, 2009, 2, 7-31.

Frank simply said: "Yes."

There are some moments in life that change your world forever. That "yes" from Frank Legge, coupled with the insights provided by Mike Rupert a few years earlier, changed mine.

My first US 9/11 related trip

In May of 2010, I became aware of a conference that was to be held in Santa Cruz, California entitled *Understanding Deep Politics*. I noted that many of the keynote speakers were people I had been reading over the years. Among them were Cynthia McKinney, David Ray Griffin and Peter Dale Scott. McKinney had been a fire-brand member of the US House of Representatives; Griffin had written many books on the 9/11 event; and Scott was the first writer to coin the phrase the "Deep State". These were people I wanted to meet. So, I booked my trip to California and off I went.

I met Scott, briefly. McKinney, it turned out, could not make it due to a family crisis. Griffin, I listened to from the audience but didn't get to actually meet. But I did meet numerous other intriguing people, including some of the other keynote speakers like Ellen Brown, the California lawyer who was championing the creation of a new banking system for the US modelled upon the Commonwealth Bank of Australia. On learning that I was Australian and had worked for three banks in my career, she was keen to query me about the Australian banking system.

Another keynote speaker at the conference was Michael Parenti. He alluded to his book *Democracy for the Few* in his talk but did not elaborate further. It is only recently that I have acquired a copy of that work and read it. It confirmed my above-mentioned thinking on this influential group. I have included a poignant quote from his 9th edition in Appendix 2 at the end of this work.

On the morning following the conference, I again met up with Ellen at breakfast. She introduced me to Carol Brouillet, a San Francisco radio personality. I had heard her name whispered around the audience over the two and a half days of the conference. Carol invited me to join a group of people who were heading up to the hills above the city, to a place called Los Gatos, for a retreat to discuss what to do, in practical terms, about the various issues that had been discussed at the conference. So, I readily agreed.

I only stayed for the first day of the retreat though. Once I realized that the group was not going to do much more than produce a document that would be posted on the internet, I did not see much point in staying. The document was produced and posted, and can still be read as the *Declaration of Accountability*. It is written in the same style as the United States Declaration of Independence with a list of grievances followed by a declaration of intention to pursue redress for those shortcomings. I left because I didn't think that would achieve much. I don't think that it has to this day.

The main reason I went to Santa Cruz, however, was to meet and personally appraise the so-called "9/11 Truthers". Were they "tin-foil-hat crazies", as some of their critics claimed, or were they sane, rational people with a serious message to share?

To my surprise, I concluded the latter. Practically all of the people I met were well-educated, articulate, sane, rational, mostly professional, people: retired university professors, journalists, architects, engineers, psychologists, and the like. They were not your average check-shirted, red-necked, UFO watching, "conspiracy theorists" that they were often described as. They were, in the main, very impressive people, and, please appreciate that, after twenty years working with the type of highly talented people that tend to lead major organizations, I was well qualified to recognize.

After leaving Santa Cruz I hired a car and drove up to Montana. There I dropped into a "gun show" where a local tried to sell me an AK47 complete with ammunition. I declined, of course. Later, I drove up to Missoula and attended the "Liberty Convention". The folks at that meet were of an entirely different breed to the Californians. The Mistress of Ceremonies explained that she had wanted to wear her six-gun but that the owners of the venue wouldn't allow her. So, her holster sported a copy of the US Constitution instead.

I had never heard of them at the time, but the venue was only a few tens of miles from the home of the "Proud Boys" – of the January 6th 2021 US Capital invasion fame – and I'm sure there must have been some of those in the audience that night. They were all "genuine American patriots", complete with a Southern Baptist preacher breathing fire and brimstone and exhorting the Lord to aid their cause. And, of course, everyone rose and sang the "Star-Spangled Banner" at the start of proceedings. I rose in respect also, but I didn't sing. Her Majesty would not have been amused.

Getting serious about 9/11 Truth

Later that year, the lead author of the abovementioned research paper, Professor Niels Harrit, came to Australia and gave a single public lecture in Sydney. Having been forewarned of the event, I flew over to Sydney from Perth specifically to attend that lecture. At the half-time interval of the event, I went up to Professor Harrit and introduced myself. The following day I also met Dr Legge in person. He had also flown over from Perth to participate in the same event.

On the way back from Sydney the following day, I commenced drafting what later became my *9/11 Research Report – an Australian Perspective*. I started off in bullet-point format, just jotting down a summary of what I had learned about the 9/11 event up to that point in time. I fleshed it out in the ensuing few months and emailed it to several people I had met through the Australian Institute of International Relations. They were polite but not encouraging.

My *9/11 Research Report* is reiterated below in subsequent reports, so to avoid repetition within this main text, I have reproduced the original in Appendix 3 to this work. It is complete with the footnotes which accompanied the original version. I'm sorry to burden you with that last mentioned academic detail, but after completing two university degrees and a graduate diploma, I have had all of that academic discipline drummed into me so that it comes as second nature to me now to add footnotes or endnotes whenever I write anything entailing serious scholarship. The report then contained a short biography of me which is available at the back of this book.

I sent that report to all major political parties in Australia in November 2010. One copy I sent to my local member of parliament, a Labor Party member, and the others to the national office of the main opposition party, the Liberal Party, and also to the state and federal offices of the Greens. I received an electronic acknowledgement from my local member acknowledging receipt of my email but nothing from the other addressees. Nor did I receive any response from my local member in respect of the content of my actual report.

In May 2011, my wife and I embarked upon another of our overseas adventures, this time to Spain, Portugal and Morocco and followed up with a week stopover in Greece. Between the former Iberian, and latter Greek, tours we spent a week in Barcelona where we met up with friends who were in Europe on similar tours.

Prior to leaving home, however, I had noticed that a Spanish engineering professor, who had written a report on 9/11, lived in that city. So, I contacted her and arranged to meet her during my visit. We did so. She came to my hotel and I arranged a meeting room for us.

The account of our meeting is reported below. It is self-explanatory. At the end of that meeting, I promised her that I would send a copy of her report directly to the prime minister's office as soon as I returned home. I did so, as promised, in late May 2011. In addition, though, I included a copy of the 2010 *9/11 Research Report* with an addendum, explaining how I obtained the authenticated copy of her report. That addendum is reproduced in Appendix 4 to this narrative. I received no response from the prime minister's office.

My advices to the Australian Federal Police

In late 2011, I attended another conference in Fremantle on national security. At lunchtime, I found myself sitting across the table from an Australian Federal Police officer. So, I told him about my meeting with Professor Carracso in Barcelona. He suggested I put that advice in writing and send it to him. I did so the following Monday morning. My email to the AFP on 14th September 2011 reads as follows:

> Hi Ross,
>
> Further to our discussion over lunch at the Fremantle security conference on Friday, I am attaching the following as promised:
>
> 1. A copy of my "9/11 Research Report – An Australian Perspective" which I e-mailed to my local MP, Mr Gary Grey, and to the national offices of the Liberal and Greens parties and to the state office of the Greens last November.
>
> 2. A copy of the Addendum to my 9/11 Research Report that I sent to the same addressees after my return from Spain in May of this year.
>
> 3. A copy of the Harrit et al "Nanothermite" paper which is referred to in item 1 of my original report. This article is considered by the 9/11 Truth movement to be the "smoking gun" which proves that explosives were used to bring down the twin towers of the World Trade

Centre (WTC) and WTC7. As my abovementioned reports shows, I have confirmed the authenticity of this report with its lead author, Professor Niels Harrit from the University of Copenhagen, and with Dr Frank Legge, an Australian co-author of the paper, who lives in Perth.

4. A copy of the English language version of a report by Professor Amparo Sacristan Carracso reporting the results of her analysis of the visual images of the aircraft that hit the South tower of the World Trade Centre on 9/11. In her report she concludes that the apparent anomalous cylindrical shapes attached to the underside of this aircraft are real physical objects. I believe that this report proves that the aircraft that hit the South Tower of the World Trade Centre was not a commercial airliner. I have personally confirmed that conclusion with Professor Carrasco in a meeting with her in Barcelona, Spain in May of this year. I also have a copy of the attached report written in Spanish which Professor Carracso signed in my presence confirming the authenticity of her report and acknowledging that she still stands by its findings.

I believe that both the Harrit et al "Nanothermite" paper and the Carrasco image analysis report constitute scientifically-based forensic evidence supporting the argument that the official United States Government explanation on what happened on 9/11 is wrong. The rest of my 9/11 report cites the secondary source evidence that I have also relied upon to arrive at my two substantive conclusions, namely:

(a) That the official United States Government's narrative on 9/11 is not believable, and

(6) That the "Controlled Demolition" hypothesis as to why World Trade Centre buildings WTC1, WTC2 and WTC7 collapsed is a more plausible explanation than the official "Pancake Collapse" hypothesis promoted in the US Government's version. Since a controlled demolition would require months of preparation, it follows that if the "Controlled Demolition" hypothesis is proved to be correct, one must also conclude that:

(i) 9/11 was not a surprise attack, and

(ii) There must have been inside help to carry out these attacks. Since WTC7 contained the New York office of the CIA and also offices of the Defense Department, the Securities and Exchange Commission and the New York emergency management office, it is reasonable to assume that access to this building, at least, would have been restricted to persons with appropriate security clearances.

Whilst this is a very sensitive diplomatic issue for Australia, it is nevertheless, I believe, an appropriate matter for the AFP to investigate given that 9/11 was undoubtedly a mass murder and that ten Australian citizens are known to have died either in New York city or in Washington DC on the 11th of September, 2001 as a result of this event.

I will be happy to elaborate further on this material should you require.

Thank you for your patience and attention last Friday.

Cheers.

David."

The business card that the officer gave me with his email address on it identified him as:

> "F/A Ross Hinscliff
> T/L Intelligence
> Perth".

I received no response from the AFP as a result of this communication.

Taking a different approach to 9/11 Truth

I have since published my *9/11 Research Report* and its *Addendum* as an Appendix to a novel that I published in 2020 entitled: *Amerissance: American Renaissance*.[3]

Amerissance was my second novel and was written mainly to report the findings of my ongoing 9/11 research in a way that I hoped would have wider appeal than just the non-fiction reports I had been writing which local publishers did not seem to be interested in publishing. The main antagonist in this second story was a group I called the "Global Security Commission" (again GSC for short) and the key antagonist was the leader of that group, a fictional character who was modelled on the late David Rockefeller.

It took me almost ten years to write this second novel mainly because my first novel was not a resounding commercial success and I could not see myself making my fortune as a writer. But the need to find an alternative approach to telling my 9/11 truth prompted me to get on and finish it.

Unfortunately, my second novel fared no better commercially than my first so I still am not expecting to become rich and famous from my writing. So now I write as a means of enlightening people as to the findings of my research – those who will read what I write, that is.

I have always been an avid reader and, of course, much of what I read influences my view of the world. I rarely read fiction.

---

[3] *Op cit;* Linellen Press; 2020; ISBN: 978-1-922343-35-2.

Mostly I read geopolitics and history because that's where my interest lies.

Having said that, however, one series of fiction that has influenced me significantly is Isaac Asimov's *Foundation* series.[4] The thing that particularly intrigued me in this narrative was a concept Asimov calls "psycho-history". The essence of this idea is that the dynamics of large human populations, and their behaviours, makes certain outcomes inevitable. According to this idea, events unfold in a way that is beyond the control of any human being or groups of human beings. They are simply inevitable because of the dynamics of human behaviour.

The notion is not as fanciful as it might initially sound, in my opinion. A read of Paul Kennedy's classic book *The Rise and Fall of Great Powers*[5] also tends to support the same notion. The demise of the European colonial empires also supports the thesis as do more contemporary works regarding the future of the American Empire; like Immanual Wallerstein's *The Decline of American Power*,[6] *After the Empire: The Breakdown of the American Order* by Emmanual Todd,[7] and half a dozen other books that fill my bookshelves alluding to the same notion of the inevitable decline of America's global dominance in contemporary world affairs.

I also have numerous works, books and articles from a wide range of sources, in my literary collection on the 9/11 event. For example, in his 2013 book *Conspiracy Theory in America*, Professor Lance de Haven-Smith lists 27 conspiracies alleged to have been carried out that include members of the American Government

---

[4] I haven't noted the reference for the three books in the series. They are *Foundation*, *Foundation and Empire* and *Second Foundation*, and are readily available through most good bookshops.
[5] *Ibid*, Random House, New York, 1987.
[6] *Ibid*, The New Press, New York, 2003.
[7] *Ibid*, Colombia University Press, New York, 2003.

and its agencies between 1798 and 2004.[8] He then rates their degree of confirmation between "high", "medium" and" low". Those he rates as "high" in recent decades include the Gulf of Tonkin incident in 1964, Watergate in 1972, the 1980 October surprise with Iran, the Iran-Contra affair in 1984-86, the disputed 2000 presidential election in Florida, the Anthrax letter attacks of 2001, Saddam Hussein's weapons of mass destruction claims in 2003 and the disputed 2004 presidential elections in Ohio[9]. One almost gets the impression that conspiracy is a normal part of U.S. politics.

It is interesting that the rationale for the second Gulf War in 2003 is mentioned but the first Gulf War in 1991 is not. In the early 2000s, I can't remember the exact year, our guest speaker at the Western Australian branch of the Australian Institute of International Affairs was an Australian lobbyist stationed in Washington by the name of Greg Copley[10]. During pre-lunch drinks, Copley told me that, after the collapse of the Soviet Union in 1989, all of the talk in Washington revolved around the question: "How do we get the Brits out of Kuwait?"

A similarly intriguing anecdote came from one of the keynote speakers at the *Understanding Deep Politics* conference in Santa Cruz in 2010, Ian Crane, whom I actually met at that event. Crane claimed to be the first civilian to be allowed to enter Kuwait after the ousting of Iraqi forces. He made the casual observation, at the time, that it looked as though the Iraqi soldiers were trying to protect the oil wells, not destroy them. He was immediately rebuked by the American sergeant escorting

---

[8] *Ibid*; University of Texas Press; Austin; Discovering America series; 2013; ISBN 978-0-292-74379-3; Table 5.1; pp210-222.
[9] *Op cit*. Table 5.1.
[10] Copley is the author of the book *The Art of Victory*; Threashold Editions, New York; 2006, which contained glowing testimonials from the likes of Alexander Haig, the former United States Secretary of State.

his oil field tour with the words: "You could get into a lot of trouble making comments like that." Then, Cranes says, the sergeant added: "What's the matter with you, Ian? Aren't we paying you enough?"

These personal anecdotal accounts are interesting, because in the lead up to the first Gulf War, the US State Department sent three clear messages to Saddam that America would not intervene in his dispute with Kuwait. The last of these messages was delivered by the American Ambassador personally. Her account of her meeting was reported in the New York Times and the full text of her report to the US Secretary of State at the time was released as part of the WikiLeaks document dump a few years later.

To a sceptic like me, it almost looks like Saddam was suckered into invading Kuwait, believing that he had been given permission from the American president to do so, but was then double-cross by George H.W. Bush. Fanciful though interpretation that might seem, the final intrigue in this little piece of speculation is given by that old "Who-done-it" maximum: "Qui Bono?", "Who benefits?" When one looks at the main outcome of the first Gulf War, the main beneficiary of that conflict was the American oil companies. They ended up getting Kuwait's vast oil reserves; the Brits were out, they were in, the British oil assets were destroyed, and the American oil field contractor Red Adair made a fortune putting out all of the fires.

A fantastic story, you might think; maybe. But when compared with all of the other skullduggery that we know the American Government has been involved in, is it so implausible – especially for a president whose family is engaged in the oil industry and who was keen to join the big league of American oil tycoons? And, of course, since George H.W. Bush was the director of the Central Intelligence Agency before he became vice-president to Ronald Reagan, he would have been fully aware of the realities of the global energy situation at the time.

De Haven-Smith rates the "Events of 9/11, 2001" as "medium" and he cites four authorities to support his judgement.[11] Of these Griffin's and Griffin and Scott's books, as cited in the footnote here, grace my bookshelf.

As noted above, I briefly met Scott in Santa Cruz in 2010 and Griffin and Mars, both cited in the footnote also, were keynote speakers at the same conference, although I did not actually meet either of them. Tarpley, I've only read. These cited volumes, plus Scott's *The Road to 9/11: Wealth, Empire and the Future of America*[12] and *The 9/11 Toronto Report: International Hearings on the events of September 11, 2001*[13] have heavily influenced my thinking of the 9/11 issue, as have dozens of other articles I have read over the past decade and a half or so.

My 2010 9/11 Research Report, plus its 2011 addendum, was essentially reiterated in 2012 under the title: *Why I believe that the Official Narrative on 9/11 is suspect*, and sometimes also: *Why I believe that the Official Narrative on 9/11 is false*. But the content of these later versions was essentially the same as the 2010 and 2011 documents. And the addressees to whom these reports were forwarded were again mainly Australian politicians with, again, a complete lack of response.

---

[11] They were: Griffin, D.R.; *The New Pearl Harbor: disturbing Questions about the Bush Administration and 9/11*. 2004, Northampton, M.A., Olive Branch Press; Tarpley, W.G., *9/11 Synthetic Terror*. 2005, Joshua Tree, CA: Progressive Press; Jones, S.E., Why Indeed Did the Buildings at the World Trade Center Collapse, in *9/11 and American Empire: Intellectuals Speak Out*, D.R. Griffin and P.D. Scott. Editors, 2007, Northampton, M.A., Olive Brach Press, 33-62; Mars, J., *Inside Job; Unmarking the 9/11 Conspiracies*. 2004, San Rafel, CA: Origin Press.

[12] *Ibid*, University of California Press, Berkley, 2007.

[13] *Ibid*, Edited by James Gourley, International Center for 9/11 Studies, ISBN-10: 1478369205.

My second US 9/11 related trip

Since those early revelations, I have continued to attempt to bring to the attention of the Australian Government, and the Australian people generally, the fact that there is substantial and persuasive evidence now available in the public domain that proves beyond reasonable doubt that the official United States Government's account of what happened in New York City and Washington D.C. on 11th September 2001 cannot possibly be true. And, again, in the main, my attempts to do so have been unsuccessful, although, I believe, the case has now been well proven.

But, by 2016, I began to wonder if the 9/11 Truth Movement was running out of steam. It did not seem to be going anywhere either here in Australia, in the United States or anywhere else in the world for that matter.

Then, in August of that year, I became aware of a conference that was being planned for the fifteenth anniversary of 9/11 in New York City. I promptly booked tickets for the conference, for my air travel and for my accommodation. But I decided to take a detour on the way. It had become customary in California to hold a 9/11 film festival in Oakland each year. The event was organized by Carol Brouillet, whom I had met in Santa Cruz and at the subsequent *Declaration of Accountability* retreat. So, I decided to detour via San Francisco to attend the festival and catch up with Carol and others I had met and knew would be attending.

I flew on to New York two days later and attended the *Justice in Focus 9/11* conference on the 11th and 12th September 2016 weekend. An account of the proceedings of the conference is included, in summary, in the first of the reports quoted below. In the main, the New York conference repeated, for an American audience, much of the material that had been presented in Toronto five years earlier.

There were several new developments between the two conferences, however.

The first significant difference was the presentation by Professor Leroy Hulsey of the preliminary finding of his study into why World Trade Center building number 7 (WTC7) collapsed (more on that later). The second was that, at New York, Justice Ferdinando Impossimato, still at that time the honorary president of the Supreme Court of Italy, was keynote speaker, whereas in Toronto he had been a panellist hearing the evidence. The latter status had given the judge the opportunity to express his own personal view about the 9/11 event.

Judge Impossimato likened 9/11 to the "strategy of tension" that had been perpetrated in his homeland during the 1960s. The strategy entailed government agents carrying out terrorist activities to frighten the local population into demanding increased security to combat a growing communist influence in the country. The Central Intelligence Agency is reputed to have collaborated with the Italian security services in conducting this activity. It included bombings in Milan and Bologna. The now late Judge Impossimato was a giant in European jurisprudence and he is probably the most senior judge to ever express an opinion on the 9/11 event. American judges will not go near the topic. I was actually privileged to meet him personally in New York.

Joining the 9/11 Truth network

The report which appears below contains a summary of the *Justice in Focus 9/11* conference. This I report in full in Appendix 5 – *Update Summary of my 9/11 Research Activities*. It reiterates much of what my previous 9/11 reports said, those reported in appendices 3 and 4, together with additional insights inserted in some points, and which updated my research activities up to the end of September 2016.

I had the privilege of meeting (the now late) Prof McQueen in Oakland at the 9/11 film festival but in New York he was a keynote speaker at that conference. I also met Mr Tony Szamboti, who is cited in the footnotes in later chapters, in New York. Mr Greg Szuladzinski, who is also cited in later footnotes, I met in Sydney in 2018.

Other interesting connections I made during my attendance at the New York conference were some of the then-current leaders of the 9/11 Truth movements. In particular, I met the then president and founder of Architects and Engineers for 9/11 Truth Inc., California architect Richard Gage; the then president of the Lawyers Committee for 9/11 Inquiry Inc.; and then secretary, later president, of Truth Outreach Incorporated, also known as the 9/11 Truth Action Project (9/11TAP). I told each of them that, if there was anything I could do to help them, they should contact me and I would do what I could to assist them.

Six months later, the president of Truth Outreach Inc. did so. He asked me if I could find out if any of the ten Australian 9/11 victim's families had accepted the Bush Administration's compensation package to 9/11 victims' families. It seems that if they had, then they had to first sign an undertaking that they would not initiate further legal action against anyone else in respect of their loss. Most victims' families had accepted the package. This left few potential litigants who the Lawyers Committee for 9/11 Inquiry Inc. could represent to pursue any legal initiatives against the suspected perpetrators of the 9/11 crimes.

I managed to ascertain that nine out of the ten Australian families had accepted the package. The tenth I was not able to contact.

That initiated a two-and-a-half-year collaboration between me and 911TAP and, although the president invited me to join the board of Truth Outreach Inc., which I declined, he did invite me to be its Australian spokesperson with the primary task of recruiting Australian supporters to the movement. I did so, but with limited success.

But I was able to assist him in his research and administrative work and even deputized for him for a few weeks when he went on leave in September 2016 and his vice-president was indisposed. That, unfortunately, was not a particularly successful effort. I don't think that some of his other board members appreciated having a foreigner directing them, especially when I criticized one of them for issuing, what appeared to me to be, an unauthorized press release that I thought did the movement more harm than good.

On his return, Bill smoothed over the ruffled feathers of the indigent board member but he instructed me to, what in my opinion, amounted to a "get back to the kitchen where you belong" type instruction. I dutifully did so and went back to working on my own Australian-focused initiatives, much to Bill's chagrin. He expressed concern on a number of occasions that my proactive attempts to bring the 9/11 Truth message to Australian decision-makers, using Truth Outreach Inc. as my authority, might provoke a complaint by Australian authorities to their American counterparts and so bring the wrath of American authorities down on his head.

I protested: "Bill," I said, "we're suing the FBI. I think they know who we are by now."

But he also pointed out that my activities had never been formally approved by the Truth Outreach Inc. board. I thought that was a bit rich since the invitation to be the Australian spokesperson for the organization had initially come from him and I had confirmed my appointment with him twice throughout 2019. I believe that I had formal approval on the grounds of the legal principal of "apparent authority". He was, after all, the president of the organization, so I believed that I was entitled to believe that he had the authority to appoint me when he had issued the initial invitation.

Apparently, Bill did not see it that way. He finally formally ordered me to "desist" in late September 2019. That ended my spokesmanship for Truth Outreach Inc. here in Australia. An account of my activities, which mainly includes my interaction with the Foreign Influence Transparency Scheme [FITS], over this later period of 2019 is reported in my next essay: *My attempts to speak Truth to Power in Australia with respect to the 9/11 Event*, which appears partially in Appendix 6 and also partially in the next chapter.

The Foreign Influence Transparency Scheme

I have assigned most of the dialogue in that last-mentioned essay to Appendix 6, but I report its two most important exchanges in the narrative immediately below. This is because it is the first time the Australian Government has admitted, in writing, that they are actively suppressing the truth about 9/11. The reply to me reported immediately below, on 30th September 2019, from the Foreign Influence Transparency Scheme [FITS] is the main reason I am writing this book. The dialogue in the appendices enables you to see exactly what they censored and eliminated, not only from their published account of my "registrations" but also from their own records of my reports to them.

Text of an email from FITS to me, dated 30th September 2019

"Dear Mr Palmer

Thank you for your email advising that you are ceasing activity with your foreign principal. We are grateful for your consistent diligence in ensuring your compliance with the scheme.

We are now in the process of finalising all your details so that your activities can be ceased on the register. To that end, we intend to make the following changes:

1. For your communications activity of 13-14 September, we intend to retain the following: "Email sent to Media Watch on 14th September 2019 reporting a broadcast of station KTVA Alaska available here:

   https://www.ktva.com/story/41015153/fire-did-not-cause-world-trade-center-building-7-collapse-uaf-study-suggests

   and emails to the National Press Club in Canberra reporting the same KTVA broadcast and also an address by the President of the Lawyers Committee for 9/11 Inquiry to the National Press Club in Washington DC on 11th September 2019 which is available here: https://www.lawyerscommitteefor9-11inquiry.org/.

   Both e-mails requested that these events be reported in Australian media. "**<u>We will delete the rest of the description</u>** [My bolding and underling here].

2. Your communications activity for 7 September and 9 September appear to refer to the distribution of the same flyer. Please confirm whether this is the case. If so, we intend to delete the activity for 9 September.

3. If they are not the same, **<u>we intend to alter your description</u>** of your communications activity from 9-29 September to read: "Commenced distribution of a flyer that reports the release of a report on 3rd September 2019 by Professor Leroy Hulsey from the University of Alaska Fairbanks arguing that

World Trade Center Building number 7 was demolished by explosives on 11th September 2001." [My bolding and underlining here].

4. On your Parliamentary Lobbying activity of 7 September, we intend to correct a minor spelling error (Marice Payne to Marise Payne).

5. **_We intend to alter your Parliamentary Lobbying activity_** of 4 September to read: 'E-mail to four Western Australian senators, to the members for Brand and Dennison advising: "I bring to your attention that the draft final report of the study into the collapse of WTC7, the third building to collapse in New York city on 9/11, by Professor Leroy Hulsey of the University of Alaska Fairbanks which is available for download here: https://www.ae9/11truth.org/wtc7." **_We intend to delete the remainder of the description_**. [My bolding and underling in this point].

The alteration of these descriptions is to ensure that they are an _appropriate length_ and are not _overly politicised_. The FITS register is for the purpose stating the activities engaged in rather than existing as a platform to spread a message or persuade an audience. We take the same approach with all registrants, regardless of their political stance. Similarly, we allow businesses to provide a factual description of their activities but do not allow them to sell or promote products on the register. [My underlining here].

Please advise your understanding of this and provide the requested information by COB Wednesday 2 October in order for us to correctly cease your *registration.*

Thank you once again for your ongoing diligence and engagement with us.

Yours faithfully

[Signature and contact details omitted]"

The spurious excuse of the wording length is demonstrated by the fact that the longest of these registrations was 483 words whereas the FITS allowed 850 words for registrants to report their activities. As for the "overly politicized" excuse, recall that the whole purpose of the FITS scheme was for Australian commentators to report the full and exact content of their communications to Australian audiences to the scheme where the content of those communications had been provided by a "foreign political organization". What else could that content be other than "political"?

I replied to this email on the same day as follows:

Text of my email to FITS on 30th September 2019 in reply

"Thank you for your advices below [above as presented here]. I can confirm that my flyer of 7th September is indeed the same flyer as used on 9th September.

As for point 3 below [above as presented here], I would point out that if you were to publish that version it would, in fact, be false and misleading. Professor Hulsey, in his report, does not say that World Trade

Center Building number 7 was demolished by explosives. He has, in fact, persistently declined to say that. What Professor Hulsey says is that the only way he could get his model of building 7 to collapse in the manner in which it was observed, as shown in numerous videos of the collapse, was to remove all of the core columns on floors 5 to 13 simultaneously and then 1.3 seconds later to remove all of the peripheral columns for the same eight floors simultaneous.

When asked at the Q&A session immediately following his presentation: "How could that happen in real life?" Professor Hulsey replied: "I'm not going to go there". It was the sponsoring organization, Architects and Engineers for 9/11 Truth Inc., that says that the only way that they know such a collapse could happen in real life is by the use of explosives. Their opinion is supported by the 3,200 architects and engineers who have signed their petition calling for a new investigation into 9/11. Thus, it is their interpretation of Hulsey's report that states that the building was demolished by the use of explosive.

The interpretation that Hulsey's report proves that 9/11 was an inside job is my interpretation. But I do not think that that is a fanciful conclusion on my part nor in the minds of my former foreign principal. I think that any reasonable person would draw that conclusion. And I think that any twelve good and true citizens sitting on a trial jury would come to the same conclusion also.

I have since reported back to Truth Outreach Inc. AKA 9/11 Truth Action Project my decision to terminate my arrangements with them. I had asked the president of that organization for a clear instruction for me to 'cease and desist from representing myself as being an official representative of, or a spokesman for, Truth Outreach Inc. AKA 9/11 Truth Action Project' if that's what he wanted me to do. He has emailed me this morning instructing me to 'desist'. His instruction seems quite clear to me and confirms my previous understanding of his position. I can supply you with copies of this correspondence if you require.

However, I have subsequently amended the headline of that 9th September flyer to: "Scientific Report proves that 9/11 was an Inside Job" which is the conclusion that I have drawn at the bottom of the flyer. I have also now removed the 9/11TAP logo from the flyer and also removed the FITS disclosure from the bottom of the document. This is the version that I will use going forward although I will await your final confirmation that I have no further obligations under the FITS act before undertaking any further outreach activities which cites 9/11TAP in any way. The other two organizations which I have cited from time to time, namely: Architects and Engineers for 9/11Truth Inc. and Lawyers Committee for 9/11 Inquiry Inc. do not, in my opinion, meet the definition of a 'foreign political organization' and, in any case, I have no direct relationship with either of them.

I appreciate your patience and courtesy throughout this exchange. For what it's worth, I did not set out to use FITS as a broadcasting medium. It [was] only when I realised that you offered the facility to post extended messages via this medium that I decided to use it for that. Quite frankly, I was surprised just how much latitude you were affording me. I didn't know if it was an oversight on your part or whether you were affording me this opportunity because I was saying things that I knew that Australian government could not say. My later posts were designed to test just how far you were prepared to let me go. I'm not displeased with the compromise you have settled for.

As far as I know, nothing that I have told you was false or misleading but I can see why you now need to be guarded. The American government would go ballistic if they thought you were publishing the truth about 9/11 on an Australian government website. That would make them very angry. And if they were to slap an arms embargo on Australia in retaliation, that would seriously affect Australia's national security, it would render the Australian Defence Force inoperative within weeks.

So, in terms of your instruction: "Please advise your understanding of this", that is my understanding of your policy. I'm not saying you're wrong, your remit is, after all, protecting Australia from foreign influence. It's just a shame that the parliament legislated to exclude the American government in its scope of the threats that we need to be wary of. But your job is to administer the laws that parliament passes so I do understand your position.

So why do I persist with this quest? Because 9/11 was a crime, a mass murder, in which ten Australian citizens lost their lives. Furthermore, we lost 41 Australian service personnel in Afghanistan, fighting a war that we should never have been involved in because that whole conflagration was based on a lie. There has never been a proper criminal investigation into this crime. That is what my former foreign principal and its associated organizations are trying to achieve.

The other reason I have been active on FITS is because it affords me a direct line of communication to ASIO and the AFP instead of the circular methods that I was using previously. It enables me to assure them that I personally do not pose a threat to anyone, **unless the truth itself be a threat**, but that at the same time it enables me to keep them abreast of a number of initiatives taking place in the USA which, if successful, and I'm quite confident that they ultimately will be, will have a significant impact upon US foreign policy and, in consequence, on Australian foreign policy [My bolding here].

The other thing that you might like to know is that, despite now formally instructing me to 'desist' speaking for 9/11TAP here in Australia, the president of that organization has reiterated his request for me to continue in my role as unpaid consultant to 9/11TAP and he has invited me to participate in their upcoming executive meetings and their upcoming board meeting. I'm still considering whether to accept those invitations.

Please advise if you require anything further from me at this time.

Sincerely,

David Frank Palmer"

A record of my registrations with the Foreign Influence Transparency Scheme (FITS) can be viewed on the FITS Public Register at the following website: Transparency Register - Transparency Register (ag.gov.au). Just click on the link marked 'Registrants' and go to page 3 to my name 'David Palmer'. Click on the 'View Details' link and read the seventeen (17) registrations I made under this scheme.

You will note that the entries altered by FITS on its public register read as they indicated they would amend them in their email of 30th September 2019 cited above. FITS have also altered my reports to them (my 'registrations') in my private account so as to record their amended versions of what my reports say, not the full text of my communications as I actually reported them and as I have cited them in Appendix 6. This latter amendment, the alteration of my reports to them, I believe, constitutes the falsification of a public record.

Texts of the flyer referred to in my FITS registrations reported above also appear in Appendix 6, namely, my flyer entitled *WTC7 Simulation Disproves NIST Report* which was subsequently changed to *Scientific Report proves that 9/11 was an Inside Job*.

Also included in Appendix 6 is a copy of a flyer I posted on numerous public notice boards in the July to September 2019 period reporting the progress of the law suits cited above that were being undertaken in the USA at that time.

The purpose of this *My attempts to speak Truth to Power in Australia with respect to the 9/11 Event* report, which was compiled by me on 6th February 2021, was to place on the published record evidence of the fact that the Australian Government and the Australian media has been informed of the truth about 9/11 but have persistently refused to acknowledge that truth, or that they have been made aware of it. You can see their response, or lack thereof, above. The response of the media has been to ignore me. The response of the Australian Government has been to censor my writing so that the main import of my reports is obscured.

The Outcome of the US Court Cases

The FBI case in Washington DC (*Lawyers Committee for 9/11 Inquiry, Inc. et al. vs Christopher A. Wray et al.*, case 1-19-cv-00824-TNM first filed 03/25/19) was dismissed by Judge Trevor N. McFadden on 3rd January 2020 on the grounds of lack of standing. In the District of Colombia Court of Appeal his judgement was affirmed by Judges Garland, Pillard and Katsas on 16th February 2021. A petition to the United States Supreme Court for a Writ of Certiorari to review the case was denied.

The Grand Jury case in New York (*Lawyers Committee for 9/11 Inquiry, Inc. et al. vs William P. Bar et al.*, case 1:19-cv-08312-PGG first filed on 10th April 2018) was dismissed on the grounds of lack of standing by Judge Paul G Gardephe on 24th March 2021. The 2nd Circuit of Court of Appeal affirmed his judgement on 5th August 2022. A petition to the United States Supreme Court for a Writ of Certiorari to review that case was also denied.

Both of those cases are therefore now at an end as far as the United States legal system is concerned. My Lawyers Committee for 9/11 Inquiry Inc. contacts, however, have advised me that they haven't given up on seeking redress via the US courts and are currently pursuing alternative approaches through the US judicial system.

Since the evidence supporting these two cases was lodged with the original petitions in each case, in the form of 60 accompanying exhibits, it means that the US courts have received a full account of the evidence which demonstrates that the official USG 9/11 narrative is false. But, because both of these cases have now been dismissed by the US courts, that evidence has never been examined or cross-examined in a court of law. **The evidence itself has not been refuted**. It has just not been heard. And since both cases have now been dismissed at appellate level, future judges may consider that there is no reason why they should consider the issue further.

My 9/11 Truth Quest continues

Given the failure of the US judicial system to progress this cause, and given my failure to have the Foreign Influence Transparency Scheme in Australia review this evidence, I now take a different approach. That approach is now described in an essay I wrote in 2023. Again, it suffers from a certain amount of repetition, as did previous reports, but I have tried to mitigate that where the text has already been cited above. That report reads as follows:

"My further attempts to speak Truth to Power in Australia with respect to the 9/11 Event

In 2020 I published a book entitled *Wondering: A Book of writings*, the last fifty pages of which contained a 'Research Reports' section. Within that section was the essay entitled *My attempts to speak Truth to Power in Australia with respect to the 9/11 Event.*

[The report then reiterates the history on my quest, in summary form, as reported in the narrative above. It then continues as follows:]

> *I have presented the aforementioned material to politicians of all major Australian parties, to public servants, to the Australian Federal Police and to the general public. It provides proof that is readily available in the public domain, that the USG's*

narrative on 9/11 cannot possibly be true and that a new investigation into the events of that day is warranted, indeed, imperative. Those presentations have mainly included emails sent to various entities, but also included hand delivered commentaries to the electoral offices of cabinet ministers of the day, including the Australian Attorney General, Defence Minister, and Foreign Minister.

None of these representations have been formally acknowledged by their addressees, save for one automated electronic response from the electoral office of my local member of parliament acknowledging the receipt of my first 2010 email.

[The report then recounts my experience with FITS as recounted above. It then continues:]

The president of Truth Outreach Inc. subsequently withdrew my authority to act as spokesperson for the 9/11 Truth Action Project in Australia so that eliminated my legal liability under the act to report my activities to FITS and that is where the matter was left to rest. The full texts of both my registrations, and FITS censored versions, are published in Wondering. I should also probably point out that Wondering was actually published in July 2021 so the reported date in this last-mentioned report is wrong although the footnote earlier in this text is correct.

My Royal Commission submission

The next opportunity to promote 9/11 Truth to an official Australian entity came in 2022 with the establishment of a Royal Commission into Defence and Veterans' Suicide. On 9th August 2022, I lodge a submission to that commission commencing with the following introduction, again reported here verbatim:

> *I submit for your consideration a copy of my latest publication, a book of writings entitled "Wondering". The first 98 pages of this document are not relevant to your inquiry but I believe the section entitled 'Research Reports' is. That section summarizes my many attempts over the past decade to bring to the attention of the Australian Government, and the Australian people generally, the fact that the official account by the United States Government of the extraordinary events that took place in New York City and in Washington DC on 11th September 2001, commonly known as 9/11, is false.*
>
> *One reason I believe that this information is relevant to your inquiry is because the official Australian Government excuse for committing Australian forces to Afghanistan was to prevent the Taliban regime from regaining control of that country, leading to them again to harbouring Islamic militants who might, once again, launch terrorist attacks against Western targets, as they are alleged to have done on 9/11.*

A second reason I believe that this information is relevant to your inquiry is because it clearly shows that the Australian Government was aware of the falsehood of the American narrative on 9/11 before it deployed Australian troops to Afghanistan, for its later deployment, at least. I know that the Australia Government was aware of it by the end of 2010 because I told them, as my report entitled "9/11 Research Report – An Australian Perspective", which I reported to Australian politicians in November of that year, clearly shows. The key points of that report are reiterated and summarised in my report entitled "Updated Summary of my 9/11 Research Activities" in the 'Research Reports' section of Wondering.

The information that I have compiled, which is summarised in my above-mention publication, demonstrates quite clearly, that the alleged 'Terrorist Attacks on the United States of America' on 9/11 were no such thing. The evidence clearly shows that the extraordinary events that took place in New York City and Washington DC on 11th September 2001 were planned, initiated and carried out by people within the United States itself, including by American citizens. There may have been a few individuals of the Islamic faith involved in those proceedings but, if so, their role was minor, perhaps even being merely as duped victims themselves. The evidence I have reported via my many reports since 2010 clearly show this to be the case.

I invite you to review the evidence as I have summarised it in my above-mention book, and to follow the information trail to those references cited therein, to obtain a more detailed understanding of that evidence. I would strongly suggest that you review the petitions to the District Court for the Southern District of New York (case 1:19-cv-08312-PGG first filed on 10th April 2018) and to the District Court for the District of Colombia (case 1-19-cv-00824 filed 03/25/19 Document 1) by the Lawyers Committee for 9/11 Inquiry Inc. which are referenced in 'Research Reports' section of the book.

More particularly, I would also draw your attention to the text of the email sent to me on 30th September 2019 by the Foreign Influence Transparency Scheme office in my essay entitled 'My attempts to speak Truth to Power in Australia with respect to the 9/11 Event', which appears in the text below. That email clearly shows that that agency actively suppressed my reports of the evidence I refer to and has actively censored my reports to them so as to obscure the full import of my registrations.

Whilst the Foreign Influence Transparency Scheme Act 2018 instructs the secretary for that scheme not to publish information that will affect National Security, you will note that that agency has also edited and censored my reports to them in my private account with them. I am not a lawyer, but to my mind, that censorship constitutes the falsification of public records. It may even constitute other serious offences. It most certainly demonstrates that a culture of 'cover up' is not confined to the Australian Defence Force.

All of the information I have reported over the years is in the public domain. I have no access to classified material. So, if this evidence has been available to me, then it is readily available to anyone else who has cared to look for it.

I have no specific knowledge of any person who has committed suicide that may have accessed this material from public sources, or from more insightful intelligence from classified sources. But it is not difficult to imagine that someone who had experienced the horrors of war, suffered personal trauma as a result, and then become aware of this evidence, might seriously be adversely impacted mentally as a result of those revelations. And it is not difficult to imagine how their mental state might further deteriorate if their own investigations, and any inquiries they may have made, to better understand why they had been deployed to a war zone on the basis of lies, had resulted in the same response from their superiors, and from the Australian Government, as mine have been.

I have no specific professional expertise in assessing how such revelations, and any official responses to their inquiries, might have impacted the mental state of any particular veteran and serving person. I can only imagine. Perhaps the Royal Commissioners can also.

I am not a veteran but I am an ex-serviceman having served two years full-time national service from 4th October, 1967 to 3rd October 1969 and five years in the emergency reserve thereafter.

My continued advocacy for truth and justice with respect to the 9/11 event is driven by my quest to ensure that Australian service personnel are not deployed to foreign wars on the basis of, now proven, falsehoods, as the evidence I now present to the Royal Commissioners clearly shows they have been.

I commend this information to you for your consideration.

The full text of the Research Reports section of Wondering appears below. However, due to the limited formatting available via this medium, I have also forwarded to your mailing address at GPO Box 3273, Sydney, NSW 2001, a copy of the printed version of the book as additional supporting material which you may find more readable than the format in which it is reproduced below (endnotes are listed in the following text at the bottom of each specific report rather than as footnotes appearing at the bottom of each page in the printed version of the book). That text reads as follows:

The submission then quotes, again verbatim, the full text of the 'Research Reports' section of Wondering. The following day I also sent the published copy of Wondering to the Royal Commission by mail.

Royal Commission delivered its interim report to the Governor General of Australia on the date specified in its letters patent. I accessed a copy of that report a week or so later. I noted that the interim report essentially misrepresented the essence of what my submission said. So, I immediately made out a Statutory Declaration which reads as follows:

Western Australia

Oaths, Affidavits and Statutory Declarations Act 2005
Statutory Declaration

I, David Frank Palmer, of [address omitted], Western Australia, 6169, retired management consultant, sincerely declare as follows:

1. On 11th August 2022, the Royal Commission into Defence and Veterans Suicide handed its Interim Report to the Governor-General of Australia.

2. In Part 2 of this report, entitled 'Lived experience: a summary of evidence and information', in paragraph 17, the report states:

'In the submissions analysed, serving and ex-serving members narrated their diverse experiences within the culture of the ADF. As the discussion below shows, many submissions provided detailed accounts of a culture of silence and "cover ups"'.

3. Endnote 4 to Part 2 cites the reference to my submission, among others, as: '4. David F Palmer, Submission, ANON-Z1E7-Q1B3-X, p [2].'

4. The quote in point 2, and reference in point 3, above is the only reference in the report to my submission to the Royal Commission of 9th August 2021 or to my book *Wondering*

which I also submitted to the commission in a supplementary submission the following day.

5. Page 2 of my submission, in the reference cited for me above, states:

6. [The Statutory Declaration then quotes the full text on my submission introduction from 'I would also draw your attention' to 'clearly shows they have been' as reported above in paragraphs six to eight of the above cited introduction].

7. As noted above, the Interim Report made no mention of the actual evidence that I had submitted. Those submissions quoted the full text of the 'Research Reports' section of my book entitled *Wondering: A book of writings*; Palmer, David F.; Linellen Press; 2021; ISBN-13: 978-1-922343-97-0, in pages 99 to 149 of that publication.

8. The bulk of those pages related to the then status of the law suits by Lawyers Committee for 9/11 Inquiry Inc. et al … [The Statutory Declaration then cites the reference details of the two law suits as cited above] …. Those cases drew attention to the extensive and persuasive evidence, presented as attachments to the original complaints, by the plaintiff/appellants, in support of those law suits, which proved beyond reasonable doubt the falsehood of the official USG narrative on 9/11.

9. The commission's Interim Report gives no indication as to whether these references and/or their accompanying evidence were followed up and examined by the Royal Commission's staff.

10. In the Interim Report, the commission defines a 'veteran' to be anyone who has served in the full-time defence force or in the reserves so, under the Royal Commission's definition, I am a veteran within the context of its inquiry.

11. I also stated in my submission that I had no particular knowledge of the mental state of any particular 'veteran' who has become aware of the evidence submitted to the Royal Commission. However, that is clearly now not the case in view of the commission's definition of a 'veteran'. I know how I feel about the Australian Government's response to my advices: exceedingly frustrated and greatly disappointed.

12. I am in regular telephone contact, usually monthly, with two current directors of the Lawyers Committee for 9/11 Inquiry Inc. so I have been able to personally verify the above information regarding the cases cited above and remain abreast of the developments in these cases and others now currently in train.

This declaration is true and I know that it is an offence to make a declaration knowing that it is false in a material particular.

This declaration is made under the *Oaths, Affidavits and Statutory Declarations Act 2005*, at [address omitted], Western Australia on 24th August, 2022."

I held onto the Statutory Declaration for over six months, not knowing quite what to do with it. But then, in early February, 2023, the Royal Commission issued a newsletter which annoyed me immensely. To me, it read like public relations waffle, the type of communication that bureaucrats tend to write when they really have no intention of doing what is asked of them. So, I angrily shot off the following email on 7th March 2023:

> *"Commissioners,*
>
> *My immediate response to your latest newsletter can be summed up in one eight letter word that begins with 'b' and ends with 's'* [later corrected to 't'].
>
> *Attached is a copy of the Statutory Declaration that I made a few days after the release of your interim report.*
>
> *I was planning to ask for an opportunity to make a personal submission to your royal commission when you come to Perth for your public hearings. I've now decided not to bother. Making submission[s] to your commission now seems to me to be a complete waste of time.*
>
> *If you really want to help serving ADF personnel, and veterans, then recommend to the government that it stop lying to [the] Australian people. We know the second Iraq War was based on lies and there is now abundant evidence to prove that the Afghan War was also based on lies. If you don't already know this, then the term 'wilful ignorance' seems appropriate here.*
>
> *Does this constitute contempt of your royal commission? I think not. You have yet to deliver your final report. I am hoping that you will remedy the error that my Stat. Dec. points out in your final report.*
>
> *What more can I say? I believe that here I am merely speaking truth to power."*

On 15th March 2023, I received the Royal Commission's reply, dated 12th March, 2023. That reply is contained in Appendix 8.

I was somewhat irritated that my communications had been again misrepresented in the said reply, but mindful of the need for me to temper my response, I waited until 24th March 2023 and then replied as follows [again this is my writing so this is an authorized disclosure]:

> *'Thank you for your response of 12th March 2023. As you can see, I have left it for a while before replying so as to avoid an unnecessarily emotional response, unlike my email of 7th March 2023 which I dispatched in haste after reading your Newsletter No. 15. Quite frankly, I lost my temper when I read that.*
>
> *With respect to your abovementioned email, you again seem to have misunderstood the essence of my complaint. I was not complaining that your Royal Commission had not reported more detail of my submission. I was complaining that your interim report misrepresented what I reported to you in that submission. Your interim report suggested that I was complaining about a culture of silence and cover up within the Australian Defence Force. I was not. I have not had anything to do with the ADF for nearly 50 years. I was complaining about a culture of silence and cover up within the Australian Government generally and by the Foreign Influence Transparency Scheme (FITS), in particularly, who actively censored my reports to them so that their records did not show the essence of the evidence I was bringing to their attention. Your misrepresentation of my submission essentially does the same thing.*
>
> *As for your offer of counselling, what is it that you*

think I need counselling for, anger management perhaps? Well, perhaps that may be appropriate since I have already confessed to losing my temper at one of your communications. Or is it that you think that I should seek counselling to help me cope with the fact that I know, for certain, that the Australian Government has been lying to me persistently, for over a decade, about the 9/11 event, the Iraq War and the Afghan war, that none of its agencies will admit the truth about these events, and that even a Royal Commission that was set up to look into the effects on veterans and ADF personnel of these events will not look into this aspect of those events?

Yes, I am extremely frustrated. Yes, I am greatly disappointed. But I can assure you that I am not suicidal. So, I don't believe that I need counselling to cope with either my frustration or my disappointment.

It might be relevant to bring to your attention, my understanding of why the Australian Government will not 'fess-up' to the truth of these events. It is contained in my reply to FITS on 30th September 2019, which is quoted in my submission to your Royal Commission and is reported in pages 134 to 135 in my book 'Wondering'. It reads:

'As far as I know, nothing that I have told you was false or misleading, but I can see why you now need to be guarded. The American government would go ballistic if they thought you were publishing the truth about 9/11 on an Australian government website. That would make them very angry. And if they were to slap an arms embargo on Australia in retaliation, that would seriously affect Australia's national security, it would render the Australian Defence Force inoperative within weeks.'

That quote seems to be particularly relevant today in light of the announcement of the new AUKUS arrangements with the US and UK.

But we in the 9/11 Truth Movement are undeterred by these developments. We are confident that truth and justice will ultimately prevail and so we press on taking advantage of every opportunity to speak our truth wherever we can. Your Royal Commission was just such an opportunity.

I have been asked by some of my American associates to pass on the message below to government officials but since I have already established a dialogue with you, and since I know that the government will only ignore such advice, as they have done so often in the past, I thought I would give it just one last shot at appealing to the sense of duty, integrity and courage of your Royal Commissioners to see if there is not some way that they could recommend to the Australian Government that it cannot just go on appeasing the American Government by staying quiet about these matters. They owe it to all ADF personnel and to all Australian veterans to speak the truth on why they are suffering as a result of their loyal service to this nation. Truth, justice and integrity demand nothing less. If a Royal Commissioner cannot speak the truth, then who in this country can?

Of the six signatories on the article below [which is not included here because it was basically a circular from Architects and Engineers for 9/11 Truth Inc. exhorting its supporters to pass on details of its recent initiatives to their congress representatives in the USA], I have exchanged emails with just one of them ... ... But I am in regular contact with the founder of this organization, American architect Richard Gage. I speak with Richard on a monthly basis via a regular teleconference with likeminded people worldwide. He is also on the board of the Lawyers Committee for 9/11 Inquiry Inc., the law firm which brought the two law suits I have referred to in my submission.

Another regular participant in those monthly teleconferences is Dr Lucy Morgan Edwards. Dr Edwards spent six years in Afghanistan between 2008 and 2014, at the same time of Australia's third deployment to that country. Lucy told me that nothing that you hear on the news about Afghanistan is anything like to lived experience of the Afghan people during those years. She is still in touch with many Afghan women to this day. On 29th August 2022, Dr Edwards addressed the United Nations Security Council. A summary of her address from the UNSC's own press release is attached (see: <u>Restrictions on Fundamental Human Rights, Especially for Women, Girls Exacerbating Bleak Humanitarian Plight in Afghanistan, Briefers Warn Security Council | UN Press</u>). Unfortunately, the actual video clip of Lucy speaking, as referenced in the attached file, does not appear to work anymore but I could ask Lucy for a copy for you to view if you are interested in seeing it.

Thank you for your time and courtesy in considering my communications. Sorry about the implied profanity in my last email."

The following day I tracked down a copy of the ten-minute video clip of Dr Edwards addressing the United Nations Security Council and forwarded it to the Royal Commission for viewing. That link is available here:

https://www.youtube.com/watch?v=ZTTRktiVhwI.

Click on the "Browse YouTube" link and pick up the commentary at the 22 minute 35 second mark.

On 28th March 2023, I received a reply from the Royal Commission to my email of 24th March, 2023, the text of which, again, I have reported below in Appendix 8, but without identifying the writer or her contact details.

On 13th April 2023, the Royal Commission issued another newsletter, its number 16. It contained the phrase: "the unauthorised disclosure of sensitive information will be a criminal offence". I managed to track down this newly created criminal offence as an amendment to the Royal Commissions Act 1902 inserted into that act as new section numbered 6OQ.

Section 6OQ makes disclosure of any information provided to the commission unable to be reported elsewhere without prior permission of the person providing the information. It does not apply to the person actually providing the information, or to people specifically authorised by that person to do so. But without authorisation the reporting of such information is made a crime punishable by a maximum penalty of a substantial fine, 200 penalty units, or 12 months imprisonment or both.

Noticing that the Royal Commission's replies to me were headed "Official: sensitive", I immediately emailed the Royal Commission asking if the criminality of unauthorised disclosures applied to the Royal Commission's replies to veterans providing it with information. I have now received a reply advising that the new section 6OQ "protections" do not apply to communications from the Royal Commission.

Since I don't know exactly what that means but since I don't have the written permission to report the Royal Commission's replies, I thought it prudent not to disclose the name and contact details of the commission's staff member sending the reply. But the text of the reply is reported in Appendix 8 below. It seems it is not just the Royal Commissions Act 1902, as amended, that is also involved in this new criminal offence but also the Crimes Act 1914, as amended, and the Privacy Act 2018, as amended, and God only knows what else. My communications to the Royal Commission are my writing and so its disclosure here is obviously a disclosure authorised by me, and hence not caught by section 6OQ.

It is interesting to note that the legislation amending the Royal Commissions Act 1902, the *Royal Commissions (Enhancing Engagement) Act 2023*, in addition to inserting the new section 6OQ, also amended the description of the commission from *Defence and Veterans Royal Commission* to *Defence and Veterans <u>Suicide</u> Royal Commission* [my underlining] emphasising that the royal commission is not interested in hearing about anything other than suicide issues; a subtle but intriguing move, and one that, to my mind, effectively amends the commission's *letters patent*. Its original letters patent included the clause:

> "j. any matter reasonably incidental to a matter referred to in paragraphs (a) to (i) [the other terms of reference] or that you believe is reasonably relevant to your inquiry."

This clause, I believe, gives the Royal Commission very broad terms of reference.

To the date of the commission's interim report, it had received over 3,200 submissions. But the parliamentary commentary accompanying the *Royal Commissions (Enhancing Engagement) Act*, the *Explanatory Memorandum* and the *Bill Digest*, cited above, also pointed out that there was a dearth of submissions from serving defence force personnel; suggesting that serving personnel feared a backlash from the high command if they complained. No doubt this is the main reason for the new amendments, the "protections" as the commission's staffer called them; to reassure serving personnel that whatever they report will be held in the strictest confidence by the commission and woe betide anyone who breaches that confidentiality.

But the effect of the amendments also significantly reduces the scope of topics that the royal commission is required to consider. It effectively negates clause "j" as cited above. The royal commission can now, legitimately, ignore much relevant information relating to the circumstances leading to serving personnel and veterans' mental trauma, such as that which I have submitted to it, as being "out of scope" from its new, effectively amended, *letters patent*.

I get the impression from this subtle change in the Royal Commission's terms of reference that it received a deluge of complaints about the Australian Defence Force, the Department of Defence, the Department of Veterans' Affairs and probably a whole lot of government and non-government agencies also; so many, in fact, that they overwhelmed the commission and its resources. It certainly prompted a request for a year-long extension of the time in which to deliver its final report. The *"Enhancing Engagement"* amendment therefore seems to be an attempt by government to put a "ringed fence" around the inquiry. To me, there seemed to be many things that the Australian government didn't want the Royal Commission looking into. No doubt my submission fell into that category. I wonder what else they heard that they didn't want to have to deal with.

It should be noted that my complaint emails were compiled and sent by me, and the commission's replies to me in response of them were received by me, before I became aware of the new legislation making unauthorised disclosure illegal via the commission's number 16 newsletter. Not that this fact seems to matter given that the criminality imposed was made retrospective in the amending legislation. I always thought the making of new laws retrospective was unconstitutional.

I had asked the Returned and Services League of Australia for assistance in drafting my submission to the Royal Commission. They declined. The local Veterans' Liaison Office said that my advices were "unproven allegations". The federal office said that they could not accommodate my advices into their submission because they were "the views of a single member" and offered no further assistance. An appeal to the federal president went unanswered.

In view of this dialogue, I have therefore decided to let the matter of appealing to this Royal Commission for truth and justice with respect to the 9/11 event rest there. It seems clear to me that the Royal Commission into Defence and Veterans Suicide has no intention of taking up the 9/11 issue as part of its remit. It obviously has no intention of challenging the legitimacy of the Australian Government's policies on the deployment of Australian Defence Force personnel to overseas wars, even though it is well aware of the fallacy of its claimed rationale for doing so, and even though the outcomes of those policies directly affect the health and well-being of those defence force personnel who unquestioningly follow orders and deploy to wherever they are ordered to go. The Royal Commission seems to now take the view that it is not its problem.

Conclusions about 9/11 Truth in Australia

What the above narrative proves is that the Australian Government is well aware of the falsehood of the official United States Government's narrative on the 9/11 event but that it has no intention of publicly declaring that fact, or in publicly contradicting the US government on this matter. The written responses of both the Foreign Influence Transparency Scheme and the Royal Commission into Defence and Veterans Suicide also confirm, in writing, that they have been made aware of this deception and that they have opted, probably on the advice of Australian security agencies, to remain silent on the issue and to cover up the Australian Government's duplicity in it.

In Australia, the recently released *National Defence: Strategic Defence Review 2023*[14] reiterates the central role of the ANZUS treaty in Australia's defence strategy. In particular, it notes:

> *"Defence's strategic objectives ... ... are to shape Australia's strategic environment, deter actions against Australia's interests, and respond with credible military force, when required,"* and that:

> *"The achievement of these objectives is beyond Defence's capabilities alone."*[15]

It also notes that:

> *"Australia does not have effective defence capabilities*

---

[14] Available at https://www.defence.gov.au/about/reviews-inquiries/defence-strategic-review.
[15] *Op cit.*; clauses 7.5 and 7.6 on p50.

relative to higher threat levels. In the present strategic circumstances, this can only be achieved by Australia working with the United States and other key partners in the maintenance of a favourable regional environment."[16]

The review also states:

"Our Alliance with the United States is becoming even more important to Australia. This will increasingly include working more closely with the United States and other partners," and: "the Australia-United States Alliance, enabled through the ANZUS Treaty, will continue to grow and adapt."[17]

And it would seem on present indications that the predictions of my 2005 Draft Master's Thesis turned out to be wrong, and that of my supervisor was right. However, according to the Strategic Defence Review:

"Our Alliance partner, the United States, is no longer the unipolar leader of the Indo-Pacific. The region has seen the return of major power strategic competition, the intensity of which should be seen as the defining feature of our region and time."[18]

In the light of such a clear indication of continued close co-operation between Australia and the United States, it seems highly unlikely that the Australian Government would confront, embarrass or contradict the United States Government on practically anything.

In the United States, the 9/11 Truth Movement persists, even now, more than twenty years after the event, because American

---

[16] *Op cit. p37 clause 4.8.*
[17] *Op cit.;* clauses 6.3 and 6.4 on p45.
[18] *Op cit.;* p17.

advocates believe that, if they can get the American Government to publicly admit that the USG's official narrative on 9/11 is false, then it will go a long way to curbing the United States aggressive, imperialistic overseas adventures; to restoring American democracy by repealing or amending the *Patriot Act*; and to making the United States of America a peaceful, friendly nation, which respects the rights and sovereignty of all other nations.

The election of Donald Trump, with his "America First" policy, seems to indicate that the American people felt, in 2016, that it was time the rest of the world start looking after itself and that American policy should be focused on the welfare of the American people at home. The fact that Trump failed to "drain the swamp" in Washington, as he promised to do, could well have been the reason for his demise. The current parlous approval rating of the Biden presidency, however, suggests that the home-focused desire may still exist. The American people may yet decide that they have had enough of carrying the burdens of empire. My Draft Master's Thesis may yet turn out to be prophetic.

Even now, research work continues in respect of the 911 event. For example, a peer review of Professor Leroy Hulsey's WTC7 study is currently being undertaken by a Technical Advisory Committee within the UK's Institution of Mechanical Engineers. The review, which will also look at other explanations for the collapse, is led by one of my monthly teleconference interlocutors, Mechanical Engineer, David Llewelyn. Their report is expected to be published late in 2023. Hulsey's full report was published in March 2020, on the University of Alaska Fairbanks website.[19]

A similar ongoing research project has recently been reported

---

[19] Available here: http://ine.uaf.edu/wtc7.

in which Professional Engineer, Wayne Coste, has re-examined the physics of the collapse of the Twin Towers of the World Trade Center by the use of nano-thermite, but focusing on the propulsive properties of that material rather than its explosive properties, a process he calls "Propelled Demolition". This subtle but important distinction explains why the noise level of the 9/11 demolitions were somewhat less than is usually experienced when normal demolition charges are used in controlled demolitions. Nano-thermite, he reports, is a material that can be tailored across a spectrum of effects ranging from mere incendiary to fully-blown explosive depending on the desired use. This tailoring, however, requires highly developed technical skills that only military grade facilities are able to achieve.[20]

No-one knows, for sure, where the breakthrough will come. It may be within the United States itself; it may be in the United Kingdom or in any one of the other United States allies (my monthly international interlocutors are spread over two North American and six Western European countries).

It might even happen here in Australia. However, given the new security arrangements between the United States and Australia, and the Australian military high command's statement that they cannot provide an appropriate level of security to the country from purely domestic sources, I think that is most unlikely.

---

[20] Reported here: https://colorado911truth.org/2023/05/the-case-for-propelled-demolition-at-the-twin-towers/.

Where to from here?

That essentially brings the saga of my attempts to bring truth and justice over the 9/11 event to the attention of the Australian Government and the Australian people up to date. Since the Royal Commission route has proved to be no more successful than all of my previous efforts, I am now left with the dilemma of where to go from here.

In retrospect, I find it amazing that when I tell this story to people, they still tend to dismiss what I am telling them as merely being the opinion of some misguided conspiracy theorist. Even if they do accept that I believe what I am telling them is true, they think I must be mistaken. Surely, they seem to reason, if it was true, then others would have brought it to their attention by now. Since they haven't, I must be wrong.

I must confess to having spent a considerable time myself, pondering whether or not I could be mistaken, years in fact, particularly back in the 2008 to 2010 period. But my trip to California in 2010, where I met several leading personalities in the 9/11 Truth Movement, convinced me that they were on to something. The people I met in Santa Cruz, and at the retreat at Los Gatos, a few days later, were not "tin-foil-hat crazies" as many people said they were. They were, for the most part, highly educated, articulate, professional people; university professors, engineers, journalists, psychologists, radio and television commentators: impressive people.

The same happened on my trip to New York in 2016 to attend the *Justice in Focus 9/11* conference. Amongst this group were again engineers, architects and, predominantly, lawyers.

One of the most impressive people that I met on that occasion was the late Mr Justice Impossimato, then honorary president of the Supreme Court of Italy. He was in no doubt that 9/11 was an "inside job".

One particular academic paper that speculates on the reason why more academics have not spoken out is given by Dr David A. Hughes from the University of Lincoln. He writes:

> "International Relations (IR) scholars uncritically accept the official narrative regarding the events of 9/11 and refuse to examine the massive body of evidence generated by the 9/11 truth movement ... A survey of the 9/11 truth literature reveals that the official 9/11 narrative cannot be supported at multiple levels ... IR scholars avoid looking at evidence regarding the events of 9/11 for several reasons. They may be taken in by the weaponized term, 'conspiracy theory'. A taboo on questioning the ruling structures of society means that individuals do not wish to fall outside the spectrum of acceptable opinion. Entertaining the possibility that 9/11 was a false flag requires Westerners to reject fundamental assumptions that they have been socialized to accept since birth. The 'War on Terror' has created a neo-McCarthyite environment in which freedom to speak out has been stifled. Yet, if IR scholars are serious about truth, the first place they need to start is 9/11 truth."[21]

> So, I have come to the conclusion that the main reason that people do not believe what I am telling them is because they have not reviewed the evidence that I have brought to their attention. They believe the official

---

[21] Hughes, David A.; 9/11 Truth and the Silence of the I.R. *Discipline*; Alternates: Global, Local, Political; 45 2; 2020.

United States Government's exhortation to, in the words of George W. Bush, "let us not entertain outrageous conspiracy theories", as though to do so would be "un-American". But if people do take the trouble to actually review the evidence that the US courts have not examined and cross-examined, they will find that that evidence is overwhelming. There is no way that the official USG's narrative on 9/11 can possibly be true. So, if it is demonstrably untrue, then there must be some other explanation for what happened in New York City and in Washington DC on 11th September 2001. And if that is the case, given that 9/11 led to so much other recent history, isn't it worthwhile finding out what that other explanation might be?

In 2020, the *911 Truth Action Project* commissioned a research study by a reputable and independent social research firm into the attitudes of the American population about 9/11. One telling question in that survey was: "Do you think that it is reasonable to be sceptical about the official story about 9/11?" In response to that question, 51% of respondents answered "Yes".[22] So being sceptical about 9/11 is neither "un-American" nor irrational. Many people are, especially amongst the young.

Many people, both in the USA, and elsewhere in the world, are beginning to have doubts about the things the US government, and their own governments, are telling them, and many people are having doubts about what is told to them by the mainstream media; and rightly so, too. As the famous quote, which is often attributed to Thomas Jefferson, erroneous

---

[22] This was a private study and not published elsewhere in full. The above result however was published on the *911 Truth Action Project*'s website at https://www.911tap.org.

according to some, says: "the price of freedom is eternal vigilance." Freedom and democracy are all about scepticism. They are not about obedience or passive acceptance of received wisdom.

My thoughts on the COVID-19 outbreak

I have mentioned, in my above reported communications, the regular monthly teleconference that I still participate in. I have mentioned, thus far, two of my interlocutors in that forum, Dr Lucy Morgan Edwards and American architect Richard Gage. Yet another I have not mentioned is acknowledged as the source of much of the detail of the unusual movements of the United States Airforce interceptors in Michael Rupert's book: *Crossing the Rubicon*.

This individual is a former member of the White House staff and so is well conversant with the inner workings of American executive government. That person, however, has not given me permission to personally attribute anything to her/him and I have respected that preferred anonymity. This is the situation in which I believe journalists refer to their source as "informed sources".

In March 2020, I asked our teleconference group: "Does anyone have any hard evidence of the origins of COVID-19?" At that time, little evidence was available in the public domain beyond opinion and speculation. However, one insight came from the informed source referred to in the previous paragraph in the form of a personal anecdote. It recounted the visit in the early 2000s to a west coast naval base by the Chief of Naval Operations for the US Navy. As senior journalist at the base, the informed source was tasked with interviewing the admiral on the completion of his visit. At the end of that interview, the said interviewer asked the off-the-record question of the admiral: "If we got into a war with China, how do you think we would go?"

The informed source said that the admiral replied: "If we got into a war with China the only way we could win would be by the use of biological weapons."

The story has stuck with me since, and influenced much of my thinking on the COVID-19 issue. So much so that, in a recent teleconference in February 2023, I asked that same informed source to confirm my recollection of it. Confirmation was given without hesitation.

The "bioweapons strike" hypothesis tends to coincide with my own previous thinking on the COVID-19 outbreak. In particular, a number of features of the origins of COVID-19 have mystified me from the start. They are:

- The centrality of Wuhan to the Chinese population distribution,

- The presence of China's only Biological Research Laboratory Level 4 (BSL4) facility in that city,

- The fact that it was well known that BSL4, and other lesser level research facilities at the site, had been working on bat-borne Corona viruses for many years,

- The heavy movement of the Chinese population over the period of Chinese New Year, the proximate timing of the initial outbreak, both throughout China and overseas, and

- The fact that the COVID-19 outbreak occurred just three weeks after the World Military Games were held in Wuhan, at which three hundred American military personnel participated, and some did so poorly as to suggest that they were not really athletes at all.

The Chinese government has pointed out that just because the outbreak of the virus occurred in Wuhan does not mean that it originated there. The fact that many biological research facilities around the world were engaged in "gain-of-function" research on SARS-type viruses, including within the United States, prior to 2014, with extensive cross-cultural collaborations between various researchers globally, suggests that its commentary on the issue is plausible.

Ron Unz of the *Unz Report* alternative media website has suggested that COVID-19 was a "bioweapons strike" by the United States on China. More specifically, Unz cites Dr Robert Kadlec, a senior Trump Administration official and longstanding bio warfare advocate, whom he quotes as saying:

> *'There is, it should be noted, one straightforward way to explain all of this, but its implications are disturbing to say the least. It is that the virus was deliberately released in China by some group or groups within the U.S. intelligence and security services. The purpose of such a release would be partly to disrupt China and partly as a live exercise for pandemic preparedness – which is, as we know, how the pandemic was in practice treated by those in the U.S. biodefence network.'*

Unz then goes on to say: "While shocking, this is not outside the bounds of possibility. Consider what Robert Kadlec wrote in a Pentagon strategy paper in 1998:

> *'Using biological weapons under the cover of an endemic or natural disease occurrence provides an attacker the potential for plausible denial. Biological warfare's potential to create significant economic loss and subsequent political instability, coupled with*

> *plausible denial, exceeds the possibilities of any other human weapon.*"[23]

Of course, one would not deploy a biological weapon of any kind unless one also had its antidote available before doing so.

In addition to Dr Robert Kadlec, I am also mindful that the Secretary of State in the Trump Administration was Mike Pompeo, a well-known warmonger, and that Trump's National Security Adviser from April 9, 2018 to September 10, 2019 was John Bolton, another well-known, and even more rabid, warmonger.

In view of these insights, and as advised above, in February 2023, when I again asked the "Does anyone have any hard evidence of the origins of COVID-19?" question, another different informed source within the teleconference group said: "Yes". He cited several pieces of relevant information which are listed immediately following. He did not provide evidence to support the commentary but I have endeavoured to locate authoritative references for the points he made and they are reported in the accompanying footnotes. The points made were:

- In late 2015, Dr Ralph Baric of the University of Northern Carolina published a paper reporting that his research team had perfected a methodology for making the SARS virus more transmissible to human beings,[24]

---

[23] Unz provides an extensive commentary in this line of thinking here: https://www.unz.com/runz/american-pravda-the-covid-epidemic-as-lab-leak-or-biowarfare/#p_1_32.

[24] Menachery, Vineet D.; Yount, Boyd L.; Debbink, Kari; Agnihothram, Sudhakar; Gralinski, Lisa E.; Plante, Jessica A.; Graham, Rachel L.; Scobey, Trevor; Ge, Xing-Yi; Donaldson, Eric F.; Randell, Scott H.; Lanzavecchia, Antonio; Marasco, Wayne A.; Shi, Zhengli-Li; Baric, Ralph S. (2015). "A SARS-like cluster of circulating bat coronaviruses shows potential for human emergence"; Nature Medicine; 21 (12); pp1508–1513.

- In 2016, Moderna had patented a vaccine for the prevention of COVID-19-type viruses,[25]

- Moderna had, up to that point, never successfully produced and marketed any therapeutic product,[26]

- In the early years of its development, Moderna was funded almost exclusively by the US Department of Defence[27], and

- Pfizer subsequently acquired its vaccine formula from Moderna.[28]

I have seen other commentary that speculates similarly, although I have not noted the references of most of those sources. However, even the briefest review of the academic literature shows that research into bat-borne corona viruses has been wide-spread throughout the world since the original

---

[25] It seems that a suite of patents were filed by Moderna between 2010 and 2016 leading to the development of its mRNA "vaccine" as reported by this article: https://www.dhakatribune.com/coronavirus/2022/08/26/moderna-sues-pfizer-for-patent-infringement-over-covid-vaccine. The complexity of the conflicting claims in respect of this Intellectual Property is highlighted here: https://www.nature.com/articles/s41587-021-00912-9.

[26] The article referred to in the previous footnote says that Moderna's mRNA "vaccine" is "its lone commercial product".

[27] The schematic referred to here: https://www.nature.com/articles/s41587-021-00912-9 notes that "Joint ownership of COVID vaccine" is between Moderna and the National Institute of Health (NIH). The following website, however, demonstrates that the Defense Advanced Project Research Agency (DAPRA) has been researching this field for decades: https://www.nature.com/articles/s41587-021-00912-9. Wikipedia reports: 'The Economist has called DARPA the agency "that shaped the modern world," and pointed out that "Moderna's COVID-19 vaccine sits alongside... [other leading technologies] ...on the list of innovations for which DARPA can claim at least partial credit."' See here: https://en.wikipedia.org/wiki/DARPA.

[28] According to Moderna's lawsuit against Pfizer; the dispute may take years to resolve.

outbreak of the SARS virus; in the United States, in China and elsewhere in the world. That suggests that the SARS-2/COVID-19 virus could have come from almost anywhere, not just from the Wuhan facility in China. Production of COVID-19 as a biological weapon therefore seems to me to be a highly plausible hypothesis, with many countries showing an interest in such weapons and their countermeasures. One particularly chilling view supporting the "bioweapon" hypothesis is presented by the above-mentioned Dr David Hughes from the University of Lincoln in a 1 hour and 18-minute video. The article containing this video also contains an extensive list of supporting references and bibliography into "biological research" around the world[29].

The "bioweapons strike" hypothesis presents an interesting third alternative hypothesis to the source of COVID-19 in addition to the two more popular "lab leak" and "naturally occurring" hypotheses that are usually debated in public fora.

A fourth alternative hypothesis, one that is entertained by some members of our monthly teleconference group, is that COVID-19 is a conspiracy by the world's leading pharmaceutical companies, particularly Pfizer, as a money-making venture via the sale of vaccines and other treatments such as anti-viral medications.

I have recently had COVID-19 and was treated with the Pfizer anti-viral *Paxlovid*. Fortunately, I live in Australia, and my treatment was paid for by the Australian Government under the Pharmaceutical Benefits Scheme (PBS). But the full price for 30 tablets of that drug for those not eligible for the PBS was A$1,114 (US$746) for 30 pills. I paid A$6.30 (US$4.22). Pfizer made a bundle from the Australian taxpayer from that prescription. Unfortunately, two weeks after testing negative to

---

[29] Hughes, David A.; *What is in the so-called COVID-19 "vaccines"? Part 1: Evidence of a Global Crime against Humanity;* International Journal of Vaccine Theory, Practice and Research; 2(2), September 3 2022; pp455-586.

COVID-19, and after the *Paxlovid* treatment, I again tested positive to the virus in a Rapid Antigen Test. I didn't bother to seek treatment for this second infection. I thought I would give my natural immunity a chance to deal with it. I tested negative after five days.

The "pharmaceutical company conspiracy" hypothesis, moreover, is alleged to have been stimulated by a few wealthy individuals within the global financial elite who are heavily invested in those pharmaceutical companies. "Global Financial Elite" is a generic term that serves little purpose in identifying any possible wrongdoers or any specific crimes. That prompted me to try and identify who these malevolent individuals might be. That resulted in me writing an essay looking at this aspect of contemporary discussions amongst our teleconference group. It is contained in Appendix 7 to this work.

I would not put all of this speculation about COVID-19 more strongly than plausible hypotheses at this point in time. But, given what I know about the 9/11 deception, none of them seem as implausible to me as many other people might think.

So, as far as the COVID-19 outbreak is concerned, and any possible conspiracy that needs to be investigated and prosecuted, of the four main hypotheses: "naturally occurring", "lab leak", "pharmaceutical company conspiracy" and "bioweapons strike", I am less convinced with "pharmaceutical company conspiracy" hypothesis than the others. My current thoughts on any such suspect dealings involving the COVID-19 event is that, if the global elite were involved, it is more likely to be a case of pursuing self-interest in response to an emerging opportunity than engaging in a criminal conspiracy.

If there was deliberate intervention with the pandemic response by the pharmaceutical industry, the suppression of viable alternative treatments to combat the initial outbreaks does, however, seem to me to be a viable explanation as part of the "pharmaceutical company conspiracy" hypothesis. The comments of a number of my teleconference colleagues contribute to this leaning, particularly by one colleague who supported his opinion with references to the Stockholm conference he attended in January 2023, which is reported in Appendix 7.

I am currently more inclined to believe that the COVID-19 outbreak is a deliberate geopolitical manoeuvre designed to restrain China, and to sustain the American Empire, the "bioweapons strike" hypothesis, than as a money-making scheme by the rich. And I think that the outbreaks in the West were likely to have been China's response to that attack. I think the "lab-leak" theory is a plausible hypothesis, apparently now gaining favour in Washington. But, again, it could also be part of the "bio-weapons strike" hypothesis as a means of deflecting the blame, a "false flag" operation, as appears to definitely have been the case with the 9/11 event. I consider the "naturally occurring" hypothesis to be the least likely cause of the outbreak.

These are notions I'm prepared to consider but I am not yet wedded to any of them. I am far less confident in my opinion on the COVID-19 issue than on the 9/11 issue and I'm open to persuasive argument on any of them if credible evidence can be presented for consideration. I don't think that sufficient such evidence has been presented to date for me to form a definitive opinion on the issue, not to my satisfaction, anyway. Evidence is emerging on a continuing basis, however, so a more definitive explanation as to the origins of the outbreak may yet surface.

My thoughts on the AUKUS security pact

A new issue that has sparked my interest is the recently announced AUKUS security arrangements, which are confirmed in the recently released *National Defence: Strategic Defence Review 2023*[30]. The new nuclear-powered submarine fleet which Australia is planning to acquire will be based, initially anyway, at Fleet Base West, which is less than 10 kilometres from where I am sitting as I write this narrative. The SSN-AUKUS submarines will not arrive for another 20 years but the first of the Virginia class boats that will precede them will arrive in within ten. In addition, US and British nuclear-powered submarines will rotate through the base regularly from here on and be permanently based there from 2027 onwards. That puts me in the blast radius of a nuclear weapon should "push-come-to-shove" over Taiwan and China decides to eliminate those threats before they can engage its own forces in that theatre.

The Australian Government assures the Australian people that none of those submarines will be nuclear armed. Yeah? Right! Both the British and American navies are going to send their most potent warships to the other side of the world without them being fully armed with their most potent weapons; just because a few Australian "peaceniks" object to their presence here. Have I got that right? In any case, the Australian Foreign

---

[30] Available here: https://www.defence.gov.au/about/reviews-inquiries/defence-strategic-review#:~:text=National%20Defence%3A%20Defence%20Strategic%20Review%202023%20The%20Defence,and%20comprehensive%20process%20for%20long-term%20and%20sustainable%20implementation.

Minister recently said: "The United States Navy neither confirms nor denies that they are carrying nuclear weapons, and we respect that." So, despite the Australian Government's assurances, it seems that its actual policy is: "They don't say, and we don't ask."

Personally, I find the AUKUS arrangements slightly absurd. Even when the full complement of eight nuclear-powered submarines is commissioned into the Australian fleet, sometime in the 2050s, that will still only leave three boats on deployment on any normal rotation. Each boat will be able to launch four torpedoes and twelve missiles before its presence is detected. That's twelve torpedoes and thirty-six missiles if three boats are on station near the target zone at the time of launch. If all are conventionally armed, that means two or three major enemy ships could be sunk, and a dozen or so ground-based targets destroyed, in Australia's first strike. How much would that hurt the firepower capability of a country like China? To China, it would be a minor irritation, like having a mosquito buzzing around your head in the middle of the night, nothing more.

Now, if those boats were nuclear armed, say with each boat carrying four W.80-type nuclear warheads on a third of each boat's missile complement, then that would give the combined might of that deployed fleet the capability of destroying the central business district of half a dozen leading cities and half a dozen key military installations; naval bases, airfields, military districts, etc. Now that is something that any great power adversary would take notice of. That would be like having a dozen mosquitos buzzing around your head in an environment where malaria or dengue fever was rife.

But what would be the cost of such a strike if carried out? The enemy response would be immediate and devastating. Every major Australian city would cease to exist, as would every major military installation in the country, both domestic and hosted. Casualties would be in the millions; perhaps a quarter of the country would die instantly; another quarter within a few months; and the remaining half would be on the verge of starvation within a year because the destruction of Australia's fuel handling systems would bring agriculture to a halt and food distribution to a standstill.

And it would not matter whether the United States honoured its nuclear guarantee and launched a retaliatory strike against the adversary, because Australia would no longer exist as a viable country. Not that I think the Americans would, of course. What would be the point of endangering their own population just to avenge an ally, no matter how loyal, if that ally no longer existed? In any case, they would not need to. The Australian first strike would have already seriously weakened their major adversary.

Perhaps the promise of such an apocalyptic scenario is sufficient to deliver the desired deterrent effect. Even without being equipped with nuclear weapons, the fact that this new "impactful projection" capability, as the Australian Defence Minister has recently described it, was available to Australia, that may be sufficient to give a major power adversary sufficient cause for pause. Nuclear weapons could be delivered to Australia within hours if a major power ally chose to arm us with them. Either the United States or the United Kingdom could enter into a nuclear hosting arrangement with Australia similar to that which the United States currently has with Germany, Italy, Belgium and the Netherlands. Perhaps the Royal Australian Navy is being "fitted for but not with" nuclear weapons.

Another intriguing aspect of the *Strategic Defence Review 2023* is the reconfiguration of the Australian army from its present two mechanized brigade – essentially desert warfare – structure into a single mechanized brigade and an enhanced amphibious warfare posture. It makes one wonder: "Who are they planning to invade": the fortified artificial islands in the South China Sea perhaps? Hardly: the current amphibious capability of the Royal Australian navy's two *Canberra*-class Landing Helicopter Dock (LHD) ships would be an inappropriate platform from which to launch an amphibious assault against a major military power within its own proximate littoral. They would be blown out of the water either by the Peoples Liberation Army Navy's surface fleet, or by China's land-based air and missile forces, before they even got close to their targets; not to mention sub-sea strikes from even a modest fleet of its conventional coastal submarines, let alone China's nuclear-powered sub-sea fleet of attack submarines.

It would be an effective force, however, against the modest military capabilities of smaller Pacific Island states, like Solomon Islands, Fiji or the other micro-states of the Pacific Island Forum. They have next to no air, missile or submarine forces and only modest land-based, light infantry-type army units. Is that what the beefed-up amphibious capabilities are for: to keep any wayward governments within the near approaches of Australia's South-West Pacific "sphere of influence" from straying too far from the Canberra line?

And the other, perhaps even more perverse suspicions that come to mind, for this somewhat cynical commentator is: what if the whole AUKUS deal is nothing but a smoke screen? What if it was never intended that Australia would acquire nuclear submarines? What if it was all just a big distraction to disguise the fact that the Australian Government had just granted basing rights to the United States, on Australian soil, so that it can establish a southern strike platform for military operations against China, should events evolve into a full-blown military confrontation between those two great powers, but it doesn't want that Australian public to make a fuss about it? Are Australians being goaded into believing they are getting something of value, in exchange for granting the USA such facilities, when, in fact, the benefits are so far off in the future that it is unlikely that those benefits will ever materialize?

It is not unusual, in defence planning, to contemplate long lead times; decades are usual. But many current commentators are suggesting that the complexity, challenges and contingencies of the AUKUS deal are so extensive that no-one, not even the military planners, has any idea of what will eventually emerge from this deal. It's almost as if the Australian Government is asking for a carte blanch to spend a lot of money without really knowing what they will be getting for it.

Maybe that's what the classified version of the *Strategic Defence Review 2023* actually says. I don't know. I don't have the appropriate security clearance to be enlightened on this matter. I guess the Australian Government believes that I don't need to know.

I am, of course, only speculating here. I can do little else given my lack of access to classified material. All I am trying to do, though, is to make sense of a publicly disclosed policy that, on the information that has been made available to me, makes no sense to me at all. That makes me think that there must be a lot more to this strategy than I, and the rest of the Australian people, are being told.

The AUKUS arrangements are now in train and still unfolding. Some commentators have suggested that the SSN-AUKUS boats are never likely to arrive given the poor delivery history of UK-built military platforms. One commentator even suggested that, once Australia embraced the Virginia-class purchase and sustainment system, Australia would be reluctant to abandon this well proven capability in exchange for an unknown, yet-to-be-developed, UK-based option. However, continuing to buy American-built boats would deny South Australia its future shipbuilding prize, so that option may not be politically viable in Australia. Obviously, though, I'm not the only cynic when it comes to this deal.

I am aware of two organizations that have recently taken up this issue. They are: the *Australian Anti-AUKUS Coalition* (AAAC) and the *Independent and Peaceful Australia Network* (IPAN). I have registered my interest with both; although I have yet to decide how involved I should become with either of them. On past experience of public protest against major geopolitical decision-making, especially when those decisions are being driven by Washington, I have my doubts that their efforts will be successful to any significant degree. But I can see that someone needs to try.

The Australian Government introduced the *Defence Legislation Amendment (Naval Nuclear Propulsion) Bill 2023* into the Australian Parliament to give legal effect to the AUKUS arrangements. It sought community input to the proposed legislation prior to debating the amendments. I lodged a submission to the parliament on 20th May 2023, in bullet point format, pointing out why I thought the arrangement was not in Australia's best interests. A copy of my submission, which I described as "talking points", is contained in Appendix 9. My submission essentially said that Australia would not need nuclear-powered submarines if its defence policy was focused on the defence of Australia rather than aligning with the United States foreign and defence policies with respect to East Asia.

Similar submissions were made by the AAAC and IPAN groups as well.

Again, this issue is continuing to unfold as this narrative goes to press.

Wrapping Up

Well, that is my story, as it has unfolded to date. In this main narrative, I have indulged in some speculation based on my intuition. My understanding of intuition is that it is the sum-total of everything that you have ever learned, whether you can specifically remember its source or not. What I'm expressing here is what I currently think, based on my "gut feeling". In the appendices attached, however, I have tried to be a little more disciplined and only report what I have actually learned as a result of thorough research, hence my inclusion of extensive footnotes where I have noted them down at the time of reading.

In the above narrative I have cited some individuals whom I have mentioned in previous published works or who have specifically given me permission to cite them here. I have also cited those whose own utterances and/or writings are already in the public domain. I have refrained from mentioning anyone who has provided me with information in confidence but has not given me specific permission to name them.

Where I have cited American sources, I have retained American spelling for those items. Where syntax and typographical errors remain in appendices I have not sought to correct them because that's how they were originally presented or published.

I now find myself wondering: "Where do I go from here?" My attempts to promote the truth, as I believe it to be, about the 9/11 event, have proved to be largely unsuccessful. Most people I broach the subject with today are not particularly interested. They tend to regard it as a matter of history and not particularly relevant to their contemporary world.

My attempt to become established as an Australian writer in any fictional genre also appears to have been largely fruitless. It certainly has not been commercially successful.

It looks like my modest aged pension is going to remain the mainstay of my financial viability into the foreseeable future.

Should I write more; if so, about what? This modest attempt has been more about explaining why and how I have arrived at this point in my quest, rather than anything else.

Should I write more fiction? I started a third novel last year but abandoned it because I felt that it had all been said before. Even the plot was a poor reiteration of things I have previously read.

How does one actually create an original thought? Is such a thing even possible? Does everyone simply draw on the ideas of those who came before? Isaac Newton certainly thought so. So did Albert Einstein. What could I write that Asimov, Sun Tzu, Machiavelli, von Clausewitz, Gene Sharp, Paul Kennedy, or any of the other writers that have inspired me over the years, have not already said?

As I ponder these questions, the words of one of my poetic efforts, *Legacy*, seem appropriate in bringing this narrative to closure:

> *"Here am I with wellness fading,*
>
> *Product of the careless years.*
>
>
> *Gone the zest of youthful vigor;*
>
> *Gone the urge to lustful zeal;*
>
> *Gone the spur of raw ambition;*
>
> *Gone the dream of heights to scale.*

Now with more genteel demeanor,
Tranquility my favored goal.
Comfort, kindness, passive transit,
The quiet search for a contented soul.

And whether peace will now prevail
Or cruel frustration overtake,
Mortality in the end will triumph
And my lifeless corpse disintegrate.

Were my efforts all in vain?
Have I well spent my time?
Surely: for I have loved and am succeeded
By progeny, whole and fine.[31]

Pondering the last three and four lines of that little ditty: "Were my efforts all in vain? Have I well spent my time?" I think I could honestly answer "No" and "Yes" respectively. Even if I have not succeeded as well as I might have hoped, at least I can claim the same retort as Jack Nicholson's character did in that classic movie "One Flew over the Cuckoo's Nest": "But at least I tried." Perhaps, like the narrative of that tale, my efforts will inspire some else to try also.

As for the progeny referred to in the last line, raising my

---

[31] *Wondering, op cit.*, above, p22.

triplets to adulthood and sending them out into the world as healthy, happy and well-adjusted citizens, well, that has been my finest achievement. And as for the journey, over the whole of my life, I believe I can again validly quote one of the classics, the song 'I did it my way' sung by Frank Sinatra: "Regrets, I've got a few, but then, too few to mention". On the whole, this thing called "My Life" has been fabulous.

Appendix 1 – My Draft Master's Thesis

This is the latest draft of my master's thesis as it stood in January 2005. It reads:

"The implications for Australia of a significant decline in American power within the foreseeable future

Introduction

In a public lecture in Perth in 2003, Professor Johan Galtung of the Norwegian Transcend Institute predicted the coming decline and fall of the American empire. In support of his prediction, he cited 15 "contradictions" which he felt could not be endured by any imperial power. He did not produce a written paper of his talk but I was to obtain from him a copy of the notes he used in the delivery of his talk. They read:

> I. *Economic Contradictions (US led system WB/IMF/WTO NYSE Pentagon)*
>
> 1. *between growth and distribution: overproduction relative to demand, 1.4 billion below $ 1/day, 100,000 die/day, 1/4 of hunger*
>
> 2. *between productive and finance economy (currency, stocks, bonds) overvalued, hence crashes, unemployment, contract work.*
>
> 3. *between production/distribution/consumption and nature: eco-crisis, depletion/pollution, global*

warming

II. *Military Contradictions (US led system NATO/TIAP/USA-Japan)*

4. between US state terrorism and terrorism: Blowback
5. between US and allies (except UK, D, Japan), saying enough
6. between US hegemony in Eurasia and the Russia India China triangle, with 40% of humanity
7. between US led NATO and EU army: The Tindemans follow-up

III. *Political Contradictions (US exceptionalism under God)*

8. between USA and the UN: The UN hitting back
9. between USA and the EU: vying for Orthodox/Muslim support

IV. *Cultural Contradictions (US triumphant plebeian culture)*

10. between US Judeo-Christianity and Islam (25% of humanity; UNSC nucleus has four Christian and none of the 56 Muslim countries).
11. between US and the oldest civilizations (Chinese, Indian, Mesopotamian, Aztec/Inca/Maya)
12. between US and European elite culture: France, Germany, etc.

V. *Social Contradictions (US led world elites vs the rest: World Economic Forum, Davos vs World Social Forum, Porto Alegre)*

13. *between state corporate elites and working classes of unemployed and contract workers. The middle classes?*

14. *between older generation and youth: Seattle, Washington, Praha, Genova and ever younger youth. The middle generation?*

15. *To this could be added: between myth and reality."*[32]

As a result of his analysis, he concluded that the American "empire" (but not the American republic) will fall within 20 years.

This lecture came as a great surprise to the writer. He, like most of his contemporaries in Western Australia, were of the view that the United States of America (the US) stands "like a colossus astride the world" at the beginning of the twenty-first century and that the first half of this century, at least, would be as much "an American century" as was the post Second World War period of the twentieth century.

So astounding to the writer was Galtung's prediction that he decided to focus this research project on inquiring into its veracity. The essential question posed in this study is the question of whether or not the US will continue to dominate the world as a global hegemon in the foreseeable future. If so, why? If not, why not? The research that is reported below documents that inquiry.

---

[32] John Galtung, "On the coming decline and fall of the American empire", Curtin University of Technology, Perth, April 9th, 2003. Also available at http://www.transnational.org/forum/meet/2004/Galtung_USempireFall.html extracted January 28, 2004.

American Global Hegemony

The United States of America (US) has dominated the world since the end of the Second World War (WWII). Even during the height of the Cold War with the Soviet Union, the US still dominated those parts of the world not under direct Soviet control or under significant Soviet influence. To be sure there was a Non-Aligned Movement comprised of states not specifically aligned to either the US or the Soviet bloc but they tended to be rather insignificant in the world geopolitical and economic spheres (for example, India was a leading non-aligned power even though it purchased significant quantities of military equipment from the Soviet Union but India did not play a major role in world geopolitics or in the world economy for most of the latter half of the twentieth century after independence from Britain).

The Soviet Union did control much of the Eurasian land mass, of course, and it, and the People's Republic of China, denied the US any significant influence in those parts of the globe under their direct control. They were also quite influential in other parts of Asia and Africa during the post WWII era particularly in the proxy wars in Vietnam, Afghanistan and southern Africa (Angola, Mozambique, etc.). They were also influential in wooing some of the Middle Eastern states such as Egypt (prior to the peace settlement with Israel) and Syria as a counterweight to US support for Israel and the Saudi Arabian monarchy.

But even during this period of (almost) strategic military parity with the US (depending on whether we are talking about the early decades of the post WWII period or the later ones and whether we are talking about the Soviet Union and China as allies or later as rivals), neither the Soviet Union nor China carried the same weight economically or culturally as the US. The US dominated the post-WWII world economically in particular through the strength of its own economy and through the institutions that largely it created such as the International Monetary Fund (IMF), the World Bank, the Bretton Woods monetary regime (up until 1973) and the General Agreement on Tariffs and Trade (GATT) (later the World Trade Organization – the WTO). For most of the latter half of the twentieth century, the US effectively ran the world.

Has that now all changed? Most informed commentators on International Relations would say 'yes' although how it has changed in somewhat in dispute. On the one hand, a small group of US commentators, those largely associated with the US right and the current Bush administration, believe that the demise of the Soviet Union and the collapse of communism in Eastern Europe, has left the US in a position of even great dominance than prior to the 1991 Soviet collapse. They believe that this new dominance heralds the dawn of a new <u>American</u> century (the 21st – to follow American dominance in the later decades of the 20th century) which will enable the US to place its visionary stamp of democracy, free market economics, individualism and human rights on the world as a whole. They see US dominance in economics and finance, science and technology, the information age and military power enabling the US to be able to reshape the world in its own image under the overarching umbrella of "Pax Americana".

Another significant body of opinion, however, argues that the US is well past its prime as a global hegemon. Reis-Smit, for example, says:

> *"I do not believe that the United States constitutes a global hegemon. A hegemon is defined in traditional international relations scholarship as a state that can define the rules of the international system. It is consensus in the field that the United States was a*

> *hegemon in international politics in the period from 1945 through to the early 1970s. And after that period, its capacity to dictate in a unilateral fashion the rules of the international system has steadily declined. Since then, the international system has become far more complex, to the point where it is extremely difficult for any state, even a state that enjoys the degree of material preponderance that the United States presently enjoys, to dictate the rule of the international system."*[33]

World Systems Theorists also believe that the US is in decline. Shannon, for example, discusses in some detail the medium- and long-term cycles noting in particular the ascendancy phase and the decline phase of the *hegemonic* cycle, the rise and fall of empires. He suggests that contemporary United States dominance features the following phases:

1897-1913/20	Ascending hegemony
1913/20-1945	Hegemonic victory
1945 – 1967	Hegemonic maturity
1967- ?	Hegemonic decline[34]

Moreover, in *The Decline of American Power*[35], Wallerstein, the founder of World Systems Theory, suggests that the beginning of the twenty-first century will feature three main "geopolitical cleavages", namely:

---

[33] Christian Reus-Smit, American Power & World Order, National Institutes Public Lecture Thursday 13 May 2004 The Hall, University House Australian National University, Canberra, Australia

[34] Thomas R. Shannon, *"An Introduction to the World-System Perspective"*, Westview Press, Boulder, Colorado, 1992.

[35] Wallerstein, Immanuel, *"The Decline of American Power"*, The New Press, New York, 2003, Chapter 13.

- **The Triadic Cleavage** – the competition for primacy between North America, Europe and Japan (or perhaps East Asia) in a traditional balance of power struggle for dominance.

- **The Davos-Porto Alegre Cleavage** – a general rejection of the capitalist market economy and corporate liberalism as the prevailing paradigm for achieving the greatest good for the greatest number and which, for Americans, Chomsky describes as the choice between "hegemony or survival"[36]. Interestingly, of this prediction, former President of the Soviet Union, Mikhail Gorbachev has noted that "gradually, we have to abandon the consumer society".[37].

- **The North-South Cleavage** – of which, Connelly and Kennedy's prophesise: "Absent major changes…. the wretched should inherit the earth by about 2025".[38] In respect of this "cleavage", the current "war on terror" might be a viewed as a manifestation of such a clash (albeit a culturally specific one – particularly if viewed from an Arab perspective). Of terrorism, Bergesen and Lizardo note:

"Terrorism …. seem(s) to appear at key transition times within the world-system—specifically, when the then-dominant state is in decline."[39]

---

[36] Naom Chomsky, *"Hegemony or Survival – American's quest for Global Dominance"*, Metropolitan Books, New York, 2003.
[37] Mikhail Gorbachev, "As the World Turns", NPQ, Winter 2004, p19.
[38] Matthew Connelly and Paul Kennedy, "Must It Be the Rest Against the West?" *The Atlantic Monthly*, December 1994, Volume 274, Number 6, pages 61-84.
[39] Albert J. Bergesen and Omar Lizardo (2004), "International Terrorism and the World-System", Sociological Theory 22:1 March, pp38-52.

Twair reports Chalmers Johnson (author of *Blowback* and *The Sorrows of Empire*) as saying that: "I am 72 years old...but, given the pace of events, I think there's a good chance I will live to see the end of the American empire"[40]

But there are many more authorities who support the US hegemonic decline theory. Their arguments have several dimensions to them. The first is the declining percentage of US economic activity to total world production from a position of absolute dominance (over 50% of Gross World Product in 1945) to around 21% of world output at the beginning of the 21st century. Secondly, further exacerbating the US economic decline is the reported precarious state of the current US economic situation particularly its current high levels of trade and fiscal deficits. Thirdly, the dependence on imported energy supplies, particularly fossil fuels, could be an Achilles heel to the US further exacerbating US trade deficits in future years. Fourthly, although the might of the US military has no peer in the global military balance at this time, many writers argue that the US is experiencing "imperial overstretch" – that is, its forces, though dominant, are stretched too thinly across the globe to enable the US to maintain its military dominance effectively. Fifthly, it is argued that recent Foreign Policy changes have led to a loss of legitimacy by the US in world affairs with a corresponding fall in global influence. Sixthly, it could be argued that the US has now embroiled itself in another foreign war which may not be winnable and could well drain US resources and weaken it further.

This discussion below will review each of these six propositions in turn and express an opinion on whether the continuation of global hegemony by the US for the next several

---

[40] Pat McDonald Twair, "Carl Boggs, Chalmers Johnson Discuss Neocon Ideology and American Empire", The Washington Report on Middle East Affairs, Jun 2004, 23, 5, Academics Research Library, page 21.

decades is likely or whether there is likely to be a significant decline in US hegemonic power over the next fifteen to twenty years.

US Economic Dominance

Firstly, the declining US economic dominance of total world production is well documented in the historical data. Rider reports:

> *"After the Second World War, and for the next twenty years or so, the United States was at the height of its economic power"*[41].

Michael Mann writes:

> *"World War II left it [the United States] with half of the world's production and its reserve currency. The US was able to appoint the directors-general of the World Bank and was given the only bloc vote in the IMF big enough to veto any policy initiative."*[42]

Todd confirms this situation noting:

> *"In 1945 the American gross national product represented more than half of all production in the world, and the overwhelming effect of this was automatic and immediate"*[43]

From that position of global dominance, the US economy has shrunk relatively to its current level of around 21% of Gross

---

[41] Christine Rider, "An Introduction to Economic History", South Western College Publishing, Cincinnati, 1995, p536.
[42] Michael Mann, "Incoherent Empire", Verso, New York, 2003, p49.
[43] Emmanuel Todd, "After the Empire: The Breakdown of the American Order", Columbia University Press, New York, 2002, p14.

World Product[44]. US dominance of the key economic institutions of the world, the IMF, the World Bank, the WTO continues, however. In the United Nations, the US is still a permanent member of the Security Council giving it a veto power over any resolution – a power that it has exercise more frequently than any other permanent member since UN foundation – but it has lost much of its influence in the General Assembly due to the huge increase of general membership in the post-WWII years through the dismantling of the European colonial empires.

US Debt

The second issue noted above is the precarious state of the current US economic situation particularly its current high levels of trade and fiscal deficits. Of these, Twair, for example, reports Johnson (again of *Blowback* and *The Sorrows of Empire* fame) as believing that:

> *"bankruptcy is what will bring an end to Pax Americana. 'The military is expensive', he [Johnson] explained, 'but we aren't paying for it. Instead, we are borrowing to finance it. And if those creditors in Asia find the Euro, for instance, more lucrative than the dollar and tell us to pay up, it's all over'"*[45]

For some writers, US debt levels are reaching alarming levels. Reporting in 1999, after an extensive study of the US trade deficit, a study by Catherine Mann concluded that:

> *"the current account imbalance is financially*

---

[44] The World Fact Book, 2003, available at http://www.bartleby.com/151/xx.html, extracted on 23rd November, 2004.

[45] Pat McDonald Twair, op cit, 21.

sustainable 'for the next two or three more years' [my emphasis] *and sees a prospect for long-term resolution of the problem through a rise in household savings in the United States and further opening of foreign markets to exports from America's highly competitive services sector".*[46]

However, in January 2004, in a paper she reported to have been accepted for publication in the Review of International Economics, she concluded that:

"although new economy services reduce the asymmetry in estimated income elasticities and contribute to raising global growth, reasonable estimates of these two structural improvements are not sufficient to stabilize the US current account deficit, in part because the share of new economy services in trade is still small."[47]

Duncan also takes up the issue of the US foreign debt, noting in particular that persistent trade deficits in recent years have lifted the US Net International Investment Position (NIIP), that is, the total value of wealth *owned* by Americans overseas minus the total value of wealth *owed* by Americans to overseas lenders and investors to a record deficit of US$2.3 trillion as at the close of fiscal 2001 – a position that had deteriorated from a balanced position in 1988 and near balance in 1995[48]. The US Bureau of Economic Analysis (BEA) confirms these figures reporting:

---

[46] Catherine L. Mann, "Is the US Trade Deficit Sustainable?", Institute for International Economics, Washington, September, 1999, pxi.

[47] Catherine Mann, "The US Current Account, New Economic Services and Implications for Sustainability", available at http://www.iie.com/publications/papers/mann0104.pdf, extracted 23rd November, 2004, p1.

[48] Richard Dincan, "The Dollars Crisis: Causes, Consequences, Cures", John Wiley & Sons (Asia) Pte Ltd, Singapore, 2003, pp21.

> "The U.S. net international investment position at yearend 2003 was a negative $2,430.7 billion (preliminary) with direct investment valued at current cost, as the value of foreign investments in the United States exceeded the value of U.S. investments abroad".[49]

However, it is not so much the magnitude of these data that is worrying, rather it is the trend. A current account deficit in the order of half a trillion dollars (US$500 billion) a year, or more, is projected well into the future (?).

In respect of the US domestic debt situation, economics educator Gerald Swanson opines:

> "One day soon, our government will suddenly run out of cash, unable to meet its payments, leaving the United States as bankrupt as any banana republic"[50].

He also writes:

> "We are far more vulnerable than most Americans realize...with a [national] debt of $7.3 trillion. If interest rates were to hit the levels we saw twenty years ago, it would take every nickel collected in income taxes just to pay the interest on our existing debt. There would be no money left for defence, or homeland security, or education, or Social Security"[51]

---

[49] Bureau of Economic Analysis, "U.S. Net International Investment Position at Yearend 2003", available at http://www.bea.doc.gov/bea/newsrel/intinvnewsrelease.htm, extracted 23rd November, 2004.

[50] Gerald J. Swanson, "America the Broke", Currency Doubleday, New York, 2004, back cover.

[51] Ibid.

Per capita, Swanson points out that every American owes $24,910 per person. But that is just the national debt cited above divided by the current population. When consumer debt is added, this rises to $31,748 per person.

But he believes that the situation is much worse than that. Despite US citizens contributing to their old age pension entitlements via the Social Security system, Swanson reports that the US government has been borrowing these funds for years and replacing them with 'non-marketable' government securities. He also claims that recent extra policy initiatives by the Bush Administration have made the situation even worse. He writes:

> *"The Bush Administration, in collusion with Congress, has obfuscated the actual cost of rebuilding Iraq (perhaps by hundreds of billions of dollars). It hid more than $100 billion of its own estimate of the future cost of Medicare drug benefits Congress passed in 2003. It 'borrows' more than $150 billion a year from the Social Security 'trust fund', magically turns the theft into federal budget revenues, and merely spend your retirement savings. By the broadest calculation yet, our nation's total future obligation, in current dollars, is at least $44.2 trillion... It means each and every American owes $150,829 in long-term tax obligations....Add our per-capita national debt to our individual consumer debt and mortgage debt, and....every single American owes $181,533. For a family of four, that's a collective obligation of $726,212....Of course, few American families own $726,212 in any form"*[52]

---

[52] *Op Cit*, pxiii

He concludes: *"To put it bluntly, this country [the United States] is facing national insolvency in the near future".53*

Swanson's dire warnings are echoed by David Walker, Comptroller General of the United States. Confirming the essential message reported above, he states:

> *"The status quo and stay-the-course approach to deficit and fiscal matters are simply aren't viable options. Tough choices will have to be made by elected officials to address the nation's large and growth fiscal gap. The ultimate alternatives to definitive and timely action not only are unattractive, they are arguably infeasible – specifically raising taxes to levels far in excess of what the American people have ever supported before; cutting total federal spending by unthinkable amounts; or further mortgaging our children's and grand children's future to an extent that our economy, our competitive position and the quality of life for Americans would be seriously threatened...Our nation has a major long-term fiscal challenge that is not going to go away and that requires serious and sustained attention."54*

This is no rabble-rouser's hyperbole – this is the most senior financial officer of the United States of America talking – it is a real problem for the USA – and for the world.

Duncan outlined how much of a problem it is for the rest of the world in a recent interview in which he explained:

---

[53] Op cit, p10.
[54] David M Walker, Truth and Transparency: The Federal Government's Financial Condition and Fiscal Condition, *Journal of Accountancy;* Apr 2004; 197, 4, 1, pg. 26

> *"The United States cannot continue going into debt to the rest of the world at the rate of $1 million a minute indefinitely. The net indebtedness of the US to the rest of the world is already approximately $3 trillion or 30% of US GDP... and it's now growing at roughly 5% of GDP per annum. The economies of most of the United States' major trading partners have grown dependent on exporting much more to the US than the US imports from them. When the United States current account imbalance returns to equilibrium and it eventually must, the era of export led growth will come to end and the world will find itself without an engine of economic growth."* [55]

In other words, not only the Japanese "economic miracle" but also those of the so-called Asian "tigers", and indeed China itself, have been possible because of the US capacity to absorb their exports. If the US is no longer able to do this, those export-dependent economies could collapse also.

The above analysis shows that the US economy, engine of world economic growth since the end of the Second World War is now in considerable trouble. It may collapse. It may not. It may have a hard landing, a 1929-style crash but it may also have a soft, prolonged decline. Either way, it is becoming increasingly obvious that the US economy cannot continue to fulfil its historical post-war role as the economic engine of the world. Nor can it afford to engage in prolonged and costly foreign military adventures.

---

[55] Interview with Richard Duncan on The Dollar Crisis: Causes Consequences Cures available **at** http://www.business-in-asia.com/dollar_crisis.html, Extracted 30th October, 2004.

Energy Imports

The third key issue raise above is the US dependence on imported energy supplies, particularly fossil fuels. Weisz[56] notes that current US energy consumption is about 100 Quads/year, roughly a quarter of the world's total demand[57]. Klare shows annual world energy consumption as at 2000 at 402.7 quadrillion BTUs (Quads) with oil comprising 157.7 Quads. This is projected to rise to 611.8 Quads by 2020 with oil comprising 224.6 Quads.[58] Klare also shows US consumption at 2000 at 19.5 million barrels per day (mbd) against a world total of 77.1 mbd rising to 24.7 mbd of a world total of 110.1 mbd by 2020.[59]

On the production side, he reports US oil reserves as at 1999 at 30.5 billion barrels of oil (bbl), just 2.9% of total world reserves and US production of 8.0 mbd[60] (41% of his above reported US consumption figure). In other words, the US currently imports nearly 60% of its oil needs and, at current production levels, would be importing over 67% by 2020. At his reported 8.0 mbd production level (which equals to 2.9 billion barrels per year), his estimate of 1999 US oil reserves would last just over 10 years. So it seems unlikely that US production could increase significantly over the 20-year forecast period to prevent this increasing dependency on imported oil from occurring.

Fortunately for the US, imports of oil are well diversified in

---

[56] Paul B. Weisz, "Basic Choices and Constraints on Long Term Energy Supplies", Physics Today, Volume 57 Issue 7, pp 47-52, July 2004.
[57] Weisz points out that it is useful to express energy magnitudes in units of the quad (Q), where $1 Q = 10^{15}$ BTU (British Thermal Units), roughly equal to 2.5×10^{14} kcal (calories) or 1.06×10^{18} joule.
[58] Michael T Klare, "Resource Wars: The New Landscape of Global Conflict". Henry Holt and Company, New York, 2001, Table 2.1, p17.
[59] Ibid. Table 2.2, p19.
[60] Ibid. Table 2.3, p45.

terms of supply. Todd[61] shows the following key sources (in millions of barrels for the 2001 year):

Country	Mbbl
Saudi Arabia	585
Venezuela	520
Mexico	498
Canada	485
Nigeria	309
Iraq	285
Angola	122
17 other countries listed	218
All other countries	453
Total 2001 Oil Imports	3,475

Interestingly, the Millennium Institute has developed a model (the Threshold 21 model) based on stock and flow methodology, constructed at a national level for the US as well as for other countries[62]. Pedercini, in a review of nine computer

---

[61] Emmanuel Todd, "After the Empire: The Breakdown of the American Order", Columbia University Press, New York, 2002, p141.

[62] Interestingly in the Frequently Asked Questions section of their website the Institute is at pains to point out that their model does not use Systems Dynamics, which they acknowledge was invented by Jay W. Forester, or that it uses the same methodology as the World3 model. However, it is also interesting to note that Gerald O. Barney, president and founder of the Millennium Institute (MI), is also listed on the membership list of the U.S. Assn. for The Club of Rome as at 25/10/1983 – see http://www.namebase.org/sources/TL.html. He has also conducted post-graduate research at MIT. In addition, Mr Matteo Pedercini - see note 77 - also now works for the MI. His web swebsiteite also says that currently he is a candidate for M.Phil. in System Dynamics at the University of Bergen, Norway. Further, the website for Dr Weishuang Qu, MI's Director of Modeling and Analysis, reports that he "has interdisciplinary skills in system dynamics, econometrics, statistics, computer programming, and

simulation models currently in use for national development policy purposes describes it as "the most useful methodological tool considered in this analysis."[63] The model for the United States is not available in the public domain (the Institute has, however, provided the T21 model for Mozambique for demonstration purposes[64]). Nevertheless, of this projection, the Institute reports:

> *"The T21-USA model results are illuminating. Assuming a continuation of the general policies that have prevailed in the United States over the past few decades, the US is projected to become increasingly dependent on foreign sources of resources, especially energy, and to continue to contribute disproportionately to the world's stream of waste and pollution, especially carbon dioxide emissions. Major reductions in the country's resource consumption and pollution production are possible with little impact on the overall economy because the US economy is so*

Monte Carlo simulation, operations research, electrical engineering, systems engineering, operations research. He has developed the Institute's generic Threshold 21 (T21) model and applied it to many countries, including: Bangladesh, Cambodia, China, Italy, Latvia, Malawi, Taiwan, Tunisia, and the United States". So Treshold 21 is not based on World3 or on Systems Dynamics? Yeah, right!

[63] Matteo Pedercini, "An assessment of Existing Computer-based Models' Potential Contributions to the Development of a Methodology for Comparing the Development Effectiveness of Large-scale Public Investment Programs in Different Locations or Socio-economic Sectors," *Working Papers in System Dynamics*, ISSN 1503-4860, Vol. 1, No. 2, University of Bergen, February 2003 available at http://www.threshold21.com/BergenReview.pdf, extracted 24th November, 2004.

[64] Available at http://www.threshold21.com/download.html, extracted 24th November, 2004. To this writer's amateur eye, this model looks remarkably like the methodologies used in the World3 model.

*wasteful."*⁶⁵

Thus, importation of oil, plus other energy resources, is likely to continue to exacerbate the US balance of trade situation, even worsen it, for the foreseeable future.

Imperial Overstretch

The fourth issue highlighted above is the prospect of the US military experiencing "imperial overstretch" – being spread too thinly across the globe to enable the US to maintain its military dominance effectively. Johnson writes:

> *"The danger I foresee is that the United States is embarked on a path not unlike that of the former Soviet Union during the 1980s. The USSR collapsed for three basic reasons – internal economic contradictions driven by ideological rigidity, imperial overstretch, and an inability to reform. Because the United States is far wealthier, it may take longer for similar afflictions to do their work. But the similarities are obvious and it is nowhere written that the United States, in its guise as an empire dominating the world, must go on forever."*⁶⁶

He also writes:

> *"Empires do not last, and their ends are usually unpleasant. Americans like me, born before World War II, have personal knowledge – in some cases, personal experience – of the collapse of at least six empires: those of Nazi Germany, imperial Japan, Great Britain, France, the Netherlands and the Soviet Union. If one includes all of the twentieth century, three more major*

---

⁶⁵ Op Cit., available at http://www.threshold21.com/region_us.html, extracted 24th November, 2004.
⁶⁶ Chalmers Johnson, "The Sorrows of Empire: Militarism, Secrecy and the End of the Republic", Metropolitan Books, New York, 2004, p13.

empires came tumbling down, the Chinese, Austro-Hungarian and Ottoman. A combination of imperial overstretch, rigid economic institutions and an inability to reform weakened all these empires, leaving them fatally vulnerable in the face of disastrous wars, many of which the empires had themselves invited. There is no reason to think that an American empire will not go the same way – and for the same reasons. If efforts at globalization delayed the beginnings of that collapse for a while, the shift to militarism and imperialism settles the issue."[67]

The "empire" to which Johnson refers is, in his words, an "empire of bases"[68] and he provides a comprehensive list of American military deployments around the world as at September, 2001 showing the number and type of personnel (military and their dependents) on a country-by-country basis. At that time, it totalled 102,561 US army, 60,315 US navy, 24,988 US Marine and 63,234 US Air Force – 251,098 military personnel in all – including deployments to Europe (mostly Germany, Italy and Britain) of 118,105 military personnel, East Asia and the Pacific (mostly Japan and the Republic of Korea) of 91,670 military personnel, Middle East (mainly Saudi Arabia, Kuwait and afloat) of 26,878 military personnel and the Western Hemisphere (mainly afloat) of 14,015 military personnel. This was, of course, before the 2003 Iraq war during which many of the above military units, particularly the major US war fighting units such as the 1st US Armoured Division were redeployed to the war zone.

---

[67] Op cit. p 310.
[68] Op Cit., Chapter 6 "An Empire of Bases", p151.

Buchanan also notes that:

> *"Another problem the president faces is that we are running out of army. With U.S. active-duty forces down to half what Ronald Reagan left us in 1989, we have troop deployments and treaty commitments President Reagan never had to honour....America is now approaching the imperial overstretch"* [69]

Harris[70], Snyder[71] and Kennedy[72] express similar opinions[73]. Paul Quintos links the imperial overstretch analogy to the current state of the US economy noting that:

> *"US Imperialism's superstructure is ultimately only as strong as its economic base. And that base is creaking."* [74]

The US Department of Defense announced in June, 2004, that "we are performing the most thorough restructuring of U.S. military forces overseas since the major elements of the U.S.

---

[69] Patrick J. Buchanan, "Approaching imperial overstretch", 21st July 2003, available at
http://www.worldnetdaily.com/news/article.asp?ARTICLE_ID=33674, extracted 12th July, 2004.

[70] Robert Harris, "Does Rome's fate await the US?" *Sunday Mail*, October 12, 2003.

[71] Jack Snyder, "Imperial Temptation," *The National Interest*, Spring 2003.

[72] Paul Kennedy, "The relative decline of America," *The Atlantic*, August, 1997.

[73] All quoted at http://www.wordspy.com/words/imperialoverstretch.asp, extracted 27th February, 2004.

[74] Paul Quintos, "Imperial Overstretch", Ecumenical Institute for Labor Education & Research, Inc. (Eiler) and Center for Ant-Imperialist Studies (CAIS), paper was delivered at the 19th International Solidarity Affair, The Pearl Manila Hotel, Manila, Philippines May 7, 2003 available at
http://www.bulatlat.com/news/3-14/3-14-pax3.html, extracted 28th February, 2004.

Cold War posture were set in 1953".[75] The restructure is guided by five key policy themes, namely:

> *Strengthen Allied Roles... to expand allied roles and build new partnerships...[and]...tailor the physical U.S. "footprint" to suit local conditions....*
>
> *Flexibility to Contend with Uncertainty...to create greater flexibility to contend with uncertainty ...[because]...we must plan to be surprised....*
>
> *Focus Within and Across Regions...we need to improve our ability to project power from one region to another and to manage forces on a global basis...*
>
> *Develop Rapidly Deployable Capabilities....because our forward-deployed forces are unlikely to fight where they're actually based, we have to make those forces rapidly deployable...[and]...be able to move smoothly into, through, and out of host nations...*
>
> *Focus on Capabilities, Not Numbers -* "*In gauging the degree of commitment the US has to a given region, the key concept is not numbers of forces or platforms we have stationed there, but the magnitude to the military capabilities we can bring to bear there rapidly.*"[76]

The essence of the new posture.... (The term 'posture' means not only bases or facilities. It encompasses also activities, relationships, legal arrangements, and surge capability[77]") is to

---

[75] Department of Defense, "As Prepared for Delivery for the House Armed Services Committee by Under Secretary of Defense for Policy Douglas J. Feith", Department of Defense, Washington, DC, Wednesday, June 23, 2004, available at
http://www.defenselink.mil/speeches/2004/sp20040623-0522.html, extracted 25th November, 2004.
[76] Ibid.
[77] Ibid.

significantly reduce the number and locations of US military personnel deployed overseas and to enhance the US military's capability to rapidly deploy overwhelming military force to almost any part of the global.

Interestingly, just such a restructure was mooted in a strategy outlined by the Washington think tank, *The Project for the New American Century*, which pointed out that Western Europe was now a stable security environment but that the US needed to remain deployed there to ensure that NATO was the predominant military institution on the continent and not an independent European Union institution. But it also recommended that:

> *"Elements of U.S. Army Europe should be redeployed to Southeast Europe, while a permanent unit should be base in the Persian Gulf region."* [78]

It's rationale for this last-mentioned recommendation was:
> *"Over the long term, Iran may well prove as large a threat to U.S. interests in the Gulf as Iraq has. And even should U.S.-Iranian relations improve retaining forward-based forces in the region would still be an essential element in U.S. security strategy given the longstanding American interests in the region."* [79]

The restructure recently announced by the Department of Defense, plus the invasion of Iraq, gives effect, among other things, to a scaling back of the US military presence in Western Europe, and to East Asia, and effectively redeploys a significant bulk of US overseas forces to the oil rich Persian Gulf region. It also maintains a military "presence" in Western Europe and East

---

[78] Thomas Donnelly (Principal author), "Rebuilding America's Defenses: Strategy, Forces and Resources for a New Century", Project for the New American Century, Washington, September, 2000, p22.
[79] Op cit., p17.

Asia to placate allies, to maintain American control over the key security institutions in each region and to deter potential challengers to US hegemony. It also redeploys the bulk of US combat capability to the continental United States where it can be maintained at the highest state of readiness for rapid deployment to any potential trouble spot in the world. The key to such a strategy is heavy lift capability (both sea and air), and to a global C^4ISR[80] of which the US has ample and unmatched capabilities.

Whether the restructure is a response to a situation of "imperial overstretch" or merely the updating for military doctrine to the realities of the new security environment can only be speculated about. So too can the question of whether or not the new posture is a result of a US need to "economise" on its military commitments in the light of its more constrained economic situation. Even more speculative, is the question of whether the initiative might not be the start of a US retreat from "empire" to a more regionally focused (Western Hemisphere) role. Whatever the main reason, the initiative will certainly throw greater responsibility upon America's allies to contribute more to their own, and to the common, defence.

Legitimacy

The fifth issue raised above was the argument that recent US Foreign Policy changes have led to a loss of legitimacy by the US in world affairs, with a corresponding fall in global influence. The National Security Strategy of the United States of America, released in September 2002, documented the new US security

---

[80] Command, control, communications, computers, intelligence, surveillance and reconnaissance.

policy for the post-9/11[81] world. It explained that "the U.S. national security strategy will be based on a distinctly American internationalism that reflects the union of our values and our national interests."[82] It boldly proclaimed: "We will actively work to bring the hope of democracy, development, free markets, and free trade to every corner of the world"[83].

But the document also contained the policy statement:

> *"The United States has long maintained the option of preemptive actions to counter a sufficient threat to our national security. The greater the threat, the greater is the risk of inaction—and the more compelling the case for taking anticipatory action to defend ourselves, even if uncertainty remains as to the time and place of the enemy's attack. To forestall or prevent such hostile acts by our adversaries, the United States will, if necessary, act preemptively."*[84]

The policy re-emphasised a key comment made in a speech to congress by President Bush shortly after the 9/11 attacks in which he declared:

> *"Every nation in every region now has a decision to make: Either you are with us or you are with the terrorists."*[85]

---

[81] 9/11 being the colloquial reference to the 11th of September 2001 – the date on which the terrorist organization, Al Qaeda launch attacks against the World Trade Centre in New York and the Pentagon building in Washington DC.

[82] Op cit., p1.

[83] Op cit., The White House, Washington, 17th September, 2002, in the transmittal letter signed by President George W. Bush introducing the policy.

[84] Op cit., p15.

[85] George W. Bush, "Transcript of President Bush's address to a joint session of Congress on Thursday night, September 20, 2001", available at http://usgovinfo.about.com/gi/dynamic/offsite.htm?site=http://www.c

Bush had flagged the introduction of the new policy early in a speech at West Point on June 1, 2002.[86]

The policy has caused consternation in diplomatic circles around the world because it flies in the faces of international law. It effectively proclaims an American right to attack any state, organization or individual that it, in its absolute discretion, believes poses a threat to American national security, whether that entity has made any aggressive moves against the US or not. Of the early West Point speech, Brzezinski notes:

> *"It is noteworthy that he [President Bush] left "the enemy" undefined, thus reserving the widest possible latitude for an arbitrary choice of target. The newly proclaimed doctrine of pre-emptive intervention did not specify what criteria would be used to determine what is terrorism, nor did it clarify under what conditions proliferation [of weapons of mass destruction] would be viewed as an evil justifying preventative military action by the United States"*[87]

He also writes:

> *"In essence, the United States was arrogating the right to identify the enemy and to strike first without seeking international consensus on a shared definition of the threat. It was replacing the established doctrine of mutually assured destruction (known as MAD) with the new concept of solitary assured destruction (which might be labelled SAD). Not surprisingly, the shift from MAD to SAD was seen by many as strategically*

---

nn.com/2001/US/09/20/gen.bush.transcript/, extracted 1st December, 2004.

[86] Reported in Zbigniew Brzezinski, "The Choice: Global Domination or Global Leadership", Basic Books, New York, 2004, p35.

[87] Op cit., p36.

regressive".[88]

The first significant manifestation of this new policy came with the invasion of Afghanistan in 2002. This intervention received widespread international support because that country was widely known to have hosted the training bases of the Al Qaeda terrorist organization which was widely believed to have been responsible for the 9/11 attacks and was believed to be the location of its leader Osama bin Laden. There was significant international support, including military support, for this operation.

The next pre-emptive intervention, albeit with host government support, was in the Southern Philippines. This was largely ignored by the world community. Other interventions in South East Asia were mooted but did not eventuate. With respect to the region, however, Acharya notes:

> *"The post September 11 regional order in Asia appears to be a quasi-hegemonic order, founded upon US military preponderance but without the conditions to ensure its legitimation. In this context, the strategic gains made by the US could be offset by the declining legitimacy of its strategic role. A strategic preponderance will not produce stable regional order unless it also acquires legitimacy."*[89]

The most recent major pre-emptive attack by the United States, however, was not widely supported. This was the invasion of Iraq. Indeed, much of the world condemned the

---

[88] Op cit., p36.
[89] Amitva Acharya, "Terrorism and Security in Asia: Redefining Regional Order?", Working Paper No. 113, Asia Research Centre, Perth, October, 2004, p7, available at http://wwwarc.murdoch.edu.au/wp/wp113.pdf, extracted 1st December 2004.

invasion, including the leading European states of France, Germany and Russia. In fact, the only states to support the invasion with military forces were the United Kingdom, Poland and Australia. Most of the rest of the world widely condemned it. When asked his opinion, United Nations secretary general, Kofi Annan said:

> *"I have indicated it was not in conformity with the UN Charter from our point of view, from the chapter point of view, it was illegal."*[90]

Todd sums up the current situation with respect to US foreign and security policy as follows:

> *"At this point in time ... the principal failure of the United States is ideological and diplomatic. Far from being on the verge of world domination, America is steadily losing control throughout the world. Far from appearing as the upstanding leader of the free world, the United States 'coalition' went to war against Iraq despite broad UN opposition and in violation of international law. The subsequent fall in legitimacy has been flagrant; however, even before trying to sell the world on the virtues of pre-emptive war, the American strategic system had begun to fall apart".*[91]

Iraq

The sixth issue highlighted above was the suggestion that the US has now embroiled itself in another foreign war which may not be winnable and could well drain US resources and weaken it

---

[90] Reported by Islam Online.net, "18 Months Later, Annan Says Iraq Invasion 'Illegal'", available at http://www.islamonline.net/English/News/2004-09/16/article01.shtml, extracted 1st December, 2004.

[91] Emmanuel Todd, "After the Empire: The Breakdown of the American Order", Columbia University Press, New York, 2002, pxix.

further. Burbach thinks so. He says:

> *"Rather than the triumph of a new imperial order, the [Iraq] war may actually accelerate the decline of U.S. hegemony .... Events in Iraq with the end of the war suggest that the U.S. occupation will be a bloody one that contributes to the sapping of U.S. global power."*[92]

McKinlay agrees. He believes "it really is a strategic disaster for the United States."[93]

And Buchanan reports:

> *"Gen. John Abizaid, who replaced Tommy Franks [as the commander of the Iraq invasion force], has contradicted Secretary of Defense Rumsfeld to declare that Iraqis are now engaged in a 'classical guerrilla-type campaign against us.' Franks thought the U.S. Army would be in Iraq two to four years at least. Gen. Barry McCaffrey predicts five to 10 years to pacify and democratise the country. Rumsfeld says the cost of occupying and rebuilding Iraq is now $4 billion a month....Yet, it is hard to recall a 20th-century guerrilla war that did not last longer or cost more than projected. And lest we forget, most of these wars were lost. The French lost in Indochina and Algeria, the Americans in Vietnam, the Israelis in Lebanon."*[94]

As at the time of writing, the Arab insurgency in Iraq continues unabated with US and coalition forces actively engaged in operations with Iraqi security forces against irregular

---

[92] Roger Burbach, "Imperial Overstretch in Iraq", Center for the Study of the Americas, Berkeley, 5th May, 2003, available at
http://www.alternatives.ca/article630.html, extracted 28th February, 2004.
[93] Michael McKinley (2004), "Target Australia", <u>Insight</u>, Special Broadcasting Service, Australia, September 14th.
[94] Ibid.

guerrilla forces comprising both dissident Iraqis (both Sunni and Shi'ite) and other sympathetic Islamic supporters from right across the Muslim world. The "mission" is far from being "accomplished".

Conclusion

Much of what has been reported in this document supports and confirms Galtung's assessment. And, if it should do so, then the security guarantee of Australia's great and power friend and ally, the USA, will disappear also. Australia will have to look to its own resources for its security and it will have to rely on its own good standing for its influence in the world, particularly in the East and South East Asian regions, those most important to Australian economic and security interests.

But the implications for future Australian security and foreign policy rest on more than just on the availability of US military and diplomatic support, as the early sections of this paper emphasise. They also rest on the viability of the whole structure of the world system and on the modern consumer orientated way of life that Australians have come to regard as normal.

If the West generally is unable to maintain its dominance of the world system so as to be able to continue to extract a disproportionate per capita share of world resources for the enjoyment of its people, then the whole Australian way of life could become untenable. The scramble to control the world's oil supplies is an important facet of that endeavour, but so too is a potential rebellion of the global South against the global North. And, as noted above, both of these may already be underway.

If a scenario involving a significant decline in US global hegemonic power was to emerge within the next decade or so, Australia may well have to reconsider and reconstitute its entire security and foreign policies. An Australia standing alone in the world would need to adopt a significantly different security and foreign policy to an Australia backed up but the world's only remaining superpower.

Is that likely? Possibly – even likely – if the above analysis is indicative? A hegemonic decline of US power would seriously weaken the West. Australia is part of the West. Even if the EU were to rise to world dominance as a hegemonic replacement for the US, it is doubtful that its dominance would be of much support to Australia. Australia's great link to Europe as a part of the British Empire ended in 1942 with the fall of Singapore. The British have no capacity to re-establish that support. The other major participants in the EU have no particular reason to even try to do so. And the other key contenders for hegemonic dominance, Japan, China (or an East Asian union of some kind or other) or India, have no particular reason to show any special favours to an ethnically and culturally alien nation like the Anglo-Celtic transplant called Australia.

In such a situation, Australia would have to modify its foreign policy to that reflecting the power and influence of a modest regional power and to pay appropriate deference to those regional powers of equal or superior might. It would need to adopt a friendly, helpful neighbour stance in almost all facets of its International Relations. And its security policy would need to be realigned with a heavy focus on a non-belligerent, non-threatening, continental defence orientation with, perhaps, slight added emphases on disaster relief capacities to support regional stability. It would probably not include a significant peace keeping role given the preference for a non-interference policy between East and South East Asian states.

This would be a considerable shift from its current posture as a loyal and supportive ally to a global superpower."

Appendix 2 - Who Governs America?

Elite, Labor, and Globalization

As Michael Parenti describes it:

> *"Those who control the wealth of society, the corporate plutocracy, exercise trusteeship over educational institutions, foundations, think tanks, publications and mass media, thereby greatly influencing society's ideological output and information flow. They also wield a power over political life far in excess of their number. They shape economic policy through the control of jobs and investments. They directly influence the electoral process with their lavish campaign contributions and lobbying, and make it their business to occupy the more important public offices or see that the persons loyal to them do."*[95]

The Ruling Class

'What we have in the United States is a plutocracy (rule by the wealthy). Not all wealthy persons are engaged in ruling. Most prefer to concentrate on other pursuits. The ruling class consists largely of politically active members of the wealthy corporate class. Most top policy is drawn from big corporations, prominent law firms, and, less frequently, from the tertiary and

---

[95] Parenti, Michael; *Democracy for the Few*, 9th Edition; Wadsworth Cengage Learning; Belmont, CA; 2011, p151, cited as footnote 1 in Parenti's book.

scientific establishments. Many are linked by social ties and common financial interests. Many attend elite schools and have worked in the same corporations.'[96]"

I elaborate further on these themes in Appendix 7 below.

---

[96] Cited by Parenti, *ibid*, as footnote 1. 'Phillip Burch Jr., Elites in American History, vols. 1-3 (Holmes and Meier, 1980, 1981); David Rothkopf, Superclass: The Global Power Elite and the world they are making (Farrar, Strauss & Giroux, 2008).'

Appendix 3 – 9/11 Research Report

"9/11 Research Report

An Australian Perspective

The following summarizes the outcome to date of my ongoing investigations into the events of 9/11, the destruction of the twin towers of the World Trade Centre in New York City on 11th September 2001 and the implications flowing therefrom:

- A peer reviewed scientific paper authored by Professor Niels Harrit and eight co-authors published in the Open Chemical Physics Journal[97] in 2009 reports that traces of a highly energetic (explosive) material known as nano-thermite was found in dust collected from four sites in Lower Manhattan shortly after the collapse of the South Tower (the earliest being 10 minutes later, two samples several hours later and the fourth sample one week later). This high technology nano-scale material is only produced in very sophisticated laboratories like the Lawrence Livermore and Los Alamos laboratories which service the American military-industrial complex.

- The twin towers (WTC 1 and WTC 2) were not the only buildings to collapse in New York City that day. A third building, WTC 7, also collapsed. It was not struck by any

---

[97] Harrit, Niels H. et al, *op cit*, note 2.

aircraft. Furthermore, WTC 7 collapsed seven hours after the collapse of the second tower (the North Tower, WTC 1) falling in a manner highly similar to that usually observed in controlled demolitions.[98] The collapse of this third building was not even mentioned in the first published report of the 9/11 Commission.

- A French language video clip entitled "Demolition Controlee" presents visual evidence indicating that all three buildings, WTC 1, WTC 2 and WTC 7, all collapsed at near free fall speed ("chute libre" in French) and concludes that "C'est un demolition controlee" – which translates as: "It was a controlled demolition".[99]

- A three-hour video record of a seminar hosted by the organizations Architects and Engineers for 9/11 Truth and Fire-fighters for 9/11 Truth in California on May 7th 2010 presents extensive evidence and expert testimony from a structural engineer, a demolition expert and a fire-fighter corroborating the evidence cited above regarding the collapsed WTC buildings. This video presentation also features the convener of Architects and Engineers for 911 Truth, American architect Richard Gage, and American fire-fighter Erik Lawyer. It is entitled "Fire-fighters, Architects and Engineers expose 9/11".[100]

- On May 16th 2010 I attended a conference in Santa Cruz, California, entitled "Understanding Deep Politics". At that conference ten keynote speakers presented

---

[98] Numerous citations including those cited in this paper. This is now a well-recorded and verified fact even from official sources.

[3] Available at http://www.dailymotion.com/video/xbhyvw_9/11-demolition-controlee_webcam. Extracted 29th June 2010.

[100] Available at http://enlightenedfilms.com/.

information confirming and corroborating much of the evidence cited above. All speakers appeared to be highly educated, highly articulate, highly credible people – retired university professors, journalists, media commentators and professional practitioners. They did not appear to me to be "crazies". A full video record of this conference is also available at a cost of US$12 so readers of this paper can also view and judge for themselves the credibility of these speakers.[101]

- I have read extensively over the past eight years articles and books on American Foreign Policy, American History, Current Affairs, and International Relations (I have over two dozen books and over a thousand articles in my library of these subjects). Two specific books relevant to the above evidence are Michael C. Ruppert's book *"Crossing the Rubicon"*[102] and David Ray Griffin and Peter Dale Scott's edition *"9/11 and American Empire: Intellectuals Speak Out"*[103]. Ruppert is a former Los Angeles Police Department narcotics investigator and at the conclusion of his book he says that if he had been in charge of a criminal investigation into the mass murders that were committed on 9/11, he believes that he has sufficient evidence to proceed with laying charges against the senior members of the Bush Administration for mass

---

[101] Available at http://enlightenedfilms.com/ at the time of first writing. Extracted 13th July, 2010. Now (at 4th April 2011) available at http://communitycurrency.org/9/11TV/deeppolitics.html for a US$30 donation. In the DVD in this series, that featuring David Ray Griffin, the camera pans to the audience several times and at a point approximately 14 minutes into that DVD the camera highlights, centre screen, an elderly attendee with white hair and white beard wearing a grey shirt. That attendee is me.

[102] New Society Publishers, Gabriola Island, 2004.

[103] Olive Branch Press, Northhampton, Mass., 2006.

murder. Griffin and Scott were both keynote speakers at the Santa Cruz conference referred to above. In their work cited here is a chapter by Professor Emeritus Steven E. Jones entitled *"Why Indeed Did the World Trade Center Buildings Collapse?"* in which he proposes that explosives were used to demolish these three buildings. Jones is also featured in a video entitled *"Nanothermite: What in the world is High-Tech Explosive Material Doing in the Dust Clouds Generated on 9/11/2001?"* This video contains the illustrated lecture given by him in Sacramento, California on 30th April, 2009.[104]

- David Ray Griffin is also the author of *"The 9/11 Commission Report: Distortions and Omissions"*. Since publishing that work, he has summarized the 115 distortions and omissions reported in that work in an article entitled *"The 9/11 Commission Report: A 571-Page Lie"*.[105]

- At a seminar co-hosted by the Lowy Institute and the Australian Institute of International Affairs at the University of Western Australia Club on 28th June 2010 I engaged in a casual conversation with another AIIA member (I won't name him since I have not obtained his permission to cite this evidence) in which I outlined my experience in Santa Cruz and opined that it looked like the United States Government was complicit in the events of 9/11. He looked at me in surprise and said:

    "Of course, everyone in France knows that. There

---

[104] Available from 9/11TV.org.
[105] Available at http://www.9/11truth.org/article.php?story=20050523112738404 Extracted: 10th August 2010.

have been two or three documentaries aired on French television showing that."

He did not elaborate on the details of those documentaries but it does appear that the French people are well-informed on the above cited evidence whereas the Australian people are largely ignorant of it. It was this casual conversation that prompted me to start searching the world wide web using the French wording for "controlled demolition", "demolition controlee", which resulted in me locating a twelve-minute video clip referred to above.[106]

1. On 17th July, 2010 I attended a lecture at the Sydney Mechanical School of Arts given by the same Professor Niels Harrit referred to above. There he reiterated the essence of his above cited paper and summarized his findings and conclusions that explosives were used in the destruction of the World Trade Centre buildings. I met Professor Harrit and spoke with him personally. His academic and professional credentials appear to be impeccable particularly in respect of the chemical evidence which forms the basis of his paper in a field in which he is an acknowledged expert. He was later joined on stage by one of the other co-authors of the paper, Dr Frank Legge, a chemist, and also by Dr David Leifer who is an architect and "incorporated" engineer and a senior lecturer at Sydney University and David Andressen who is a civil engineer. They also confirmed Professor Harrit's conclusions.

---

[106] Available at http://www.dailymotion.com/video/xbhyvw_9/11-demolition-controlee_webcam. Extracted 29th June, 2010.

On 18th July 2010 I accepted an invitation from Mr John Bursill, a licensed aircraft engineer, to a barbeque at his home in Helensburgh, N.S.W. Mr Bursill is a member and key spokesperson of the organization Architects and Engineers for 9/11 Truth in Australia and was also the convenor of Professor Harrit's lecture. He is employed by QANTAS and specializes in avionics for Boeing 767/737 and 747 aircraft. At that barbeque Mr Bursill introduced me to several other members of AE9/11Truth movement. Dr Legge was also present. All in attendance generally corroborated the conclusions outlined above regarding the controlled demolition hypothesis. The group declined to speculate on who might have been responsible for 9/11 preferring instead to concentrate only on that evidence that they believe can be proved scientifically. However, subsequently in a review of this paper Dr Legge commented: "Although we don't say who did it, we are not afraid to point out the impossibility of gaining the necessary prolonged access without inside help."[107]

2. On the question of how could conspirators gain access to the World Trade Center buildings for all the months that would be required to place explosives, American chemist Kevin Ryan[108] has analysed the tenancy lists of all three buildings in the years and months prior to 9/11.

---

[107] Review note to the author from Dr Legge on 11th August, 2010.
[108] Kevin Ryan was actually employed at the time of the 9/11 events by Underwriters Laboratories Inc., the company that certified the steel that was used in the construction of the Twin Towers of the World Trade Center in New York, in their subsidiary Environmental Health Laboratories Inc.

In a four-part paper entitled *"Demolition access to the World Trade Center towers"* he outlines the extensive interconnection between the tenants, service providers, contractors and renovators that had access to all three buildings in the years and months before 9/11. The close affiliations of these organizations to the Bush Administration and to the US military-industrial complex are striking.

He also points out that many floors in the Twin Towers had renovation work done on them in the months and years prior to 9/11 and that a major overhaul of the central lift systems was also conducted during this period. He concludes:

"If we look at the companies that occupied the impact zones of the WTC towers, and other floors that might have played a useful role in the demolition of the towers, we see connections to organizations that had access to explosive materials, and to the expertise required to use explosives." And:

"It seems that, if certain management representatives of the tenant companies listed above wanted to help bring the WTC towers down, they would have been well suited to do so. The companies mentioned were located at well-spaced intervals in the buildings, and some ... had a reputation of being secretive. In fact, a number of the executives from these firms were either on the board of intelligence firms ... or were closely related to others who were. Others were connected to the CIA itself, and to some of the largest defense contractors in the world, like Lockheed Martin, Raytheon, General Dynamics,

Halliburton, and SAIC.

There are also strong connections to those who benefited from the 9/11 attacks, most notably the Bush family and their corporate network, including Dresser Industries (now Halliburton) and UBS, and to Deutsche Bank and its subsidiaries, reported to have brokered the insider trading deals. There are links between these tenant companies and the terrorist-related fraudulent bank BCCI."[109]

With respect of WTC 7, Wikipedia reports:

"At the time of the September 11, 2001 attacks, Salomon Smith Barney was by far the largest tenant in 7 World Trade Center, occupying 1,202,900 sq ft (111,750 m²) (64 percent of the building) which included floors 28–45. Other major tenants included ITT Hartford Insurance Group (122,590 sq ft/11,400 m²), American Express Bank International (106,117 sq ft/9,900 m²), Standard Chartered Bank (111,398 sq ft/10,350 m²), and the Securities and Exchange Commission (106,117 sq ft/9,850 m²). Smaller tenants included the Internal Revenue Service Regional Council (90,430 sq ft/8,400 m²) and the United States Secret Service (85,343 sq ft/7,900 m²). The smallest tenants included the New York City Office of Emergency Management, National Association of Insurance Commissioners, Federal Home Loan Bank, First State Management Group Inc., Provident Financial Management, and the Immigration

---

[109] Ryan, Kevin R., "Demolition access to the World Trade Center towers: Part one – Tenants", available at
http://911review.com/articles/ryan/demolition_access_p1.html
Extracted 27th July, 2010.

and Naturalization Service. The Department of Defense (DOD) and Central Intelligence Agency (CIA) shared the 25th floor with the IRS. Floors 46–47 were mechanical floors, as were the bottom six floors and part of the seventh floor."[110]

With the CIA's New York office, Defense Department offices and the Securities and Exchange Commission tenanted in the building one can presume that this was one of the most secure buildings in the city, accessible only to those with appropriate security clearances.

3. It seems that it is not just the French that are better informed than the Australians on this issue. Woodworth reports eighteen case studies of main stream media coverage being given to the 9/11 Truth Movement in Britain, Canada, Denmark, France, the Netherlands, New Zealand, Norway, and Russia. She concludes:

"This more open approach taken in the international media ... might be a sign that worldwide public and corporate media organizations are positioning themselves, and preparing their audiences, for a possible revelation of the truth of the claim that forces within the US government were complicit in the attacks – a revelation that would call into question the publicly given rationale for the military operations in Iraq, Afghanistan, and Pakistan.

The evidence now being explored in the international media may pave the way for the US media to take an in-

---

[110] Available at http://en.wikipedia.org/wiki/7_World_Trade_Center. Extracted 28th September 2010.

depth look at the implications of what is now known about 9/11, and to re-examine the country's foreign and domestic policies in the light of this knowledge."[111]

The above research leads me to conclude, with a high degree of confidence, that:

a. The official version of the events of 9/11 by the United States Government, and particularly its key instruments in the matter, the Fire and Emergency Management Authority (FEMA) report on 9/11, the National Institute for Standards and Technology (NIST) report on 9/11 and the 9/11 Commission report, are, at least, inadequate, if not a complete whitewash. They are simply incredible – that is, not believable.

b. An alternative hypothesis that the collapse of WTC 1, WTC 2 and WTC 7 was due to a controlled demolition is at least as credible as the official version – in fact, more so, in the light of the Harrit paper and the other evidence cited above.

Less certain are any conclusions that might be drawn with confidence about who might have been responsible for this crime although the above evidence suggests that some agencies of the United States Government may have been involved in some way.

Since this issue is so important to the future governance of the United States of America and to International Relations generally, a new, fully independent, competently staffed and objective investigation of the events of 9/11 is needed. This

---

[111] Available at
http://www.globalresearch.ca/index.php?aid=17624&context=va. *Extracted 26th July 2010.*

investigation needs the powers of subpoena, to take evidence under oath and to have authority to investigate deep into the American political and national security establishment. Anything less will only serve to perpetuate the ongoing distrust of the American Government – the former Bush Administration in particular but also its successor the Obama Administration and also the legislative and judicial arms of the American Government. It will also continue to foster distrust of those governments allied to the United States including the Australian Government.

The implications of the above evidence are extremely serious for Australia. The whole of Australia's Foreign Policy posture and its Defence strategy is built around the ANZUS alliance. Therefore, the maintenance of good, co-operative relations with the United States of America is vital to Australia's national security. However, it is also incumbent upon the Australia's national government to defend its citizens and to seek justice for those who have been wronged by other governments. Ten Australians are known to have died in the events relating to 9/11 in New York and Washington on that day. Moreover, Australia has participated, and is still participating, in two wars since 9/11 which have been justified on the basis that it was Islamic extremists who were solely responsible for this crime whereas the above evidence strongly suggests that this is not so.

Whilst this is undoubtedly an embarrassing, difficult and unpalatable issue for the Australian Government, Australia cannot proceed in its relations with the United States, or any other government for that matter, on the basis that some of our citizens are expendable in the pursuit of our national goals and aspirations or those of our allies. All Australian lives must be protected and defended by our government no matter what the cost or discomfort of doing so. Australia's credibility is also at stake here since it is evident that the above information has now been widely disseminated in Europe and is well understood throughout the Islamic world even if Australians and Americans are still mostly ignorant of it."

Appendix 4 – 9/11 Report Addendum

"9/11 Research Report – An Australian Perspective (Addendum)"

Further to my 9/11 Research Report that I first penned in July 2010 and selectively distributed in November 2010 I now report two further developments in my ongoing research into the events of 11th September 2001 in New York City and Washington DC:

1. On 13th November 2010 I was invited to the home of Dr Frank Legge, a co-author of the Harrit/Jones nano-thermite paper referred to in my earlier report. Dr Legge personally reaffirmed the findings of that paper and his belief in its integrity and he persuasively answered all of my questions about its findings.

2. On 4th May 2011 I met Professor Amparo Sacristian Carrasco at the Hotel Universal Barcelona in Spain. At that meeting I showed her the Spanish language version of her report of 26th March 2003 entitled (in English) "Analysis of the Images of 11 September 2001" and asked her if the report was an accurate version of her original. She said that it was. I then showed her the English language version of the report and asked her if it was an accurate translation of the Spanish version. Apart from a small typographical error (SR RR erroneously transcribed as RR) she said that it was. I then

asked her if she had had any reason to change her opinion or the conclusions of her original report in the seven years since writing it. She said "no". I then asked her if she would confirm the authenticity of her report and that she still stands by its findings by signing the Spanish language version that I had shown her. She agreed to do so and signed the report in my presence. I now have that signed copy next to me as I write this addendum.

I then asked Professor Carrasco if she appreciated the implications of her report – that it effectively proves that the aircraft that struck the South Tower of the World Trade Centre on 9/11 was not a commercial airliner. She said "yes". In fact, the only thing that she seemed perplexed about was that anyone should be interested in inquiring into this matter so long after she had completed her report. She considered it to be ancient history. This further suggests that Europeans generally are well acquainted with the information contained in my earlier paper and have difficulty understanding why others are not also as well informed.

For those readers not familiar with Professor Carrasco's abovementioned report, the English language translation of it is available at http://www.amics21.com/9/11/report.html. The Spanish language version is available by hypertext link from that document also. The report confirms that the apparent cylindrical shapes noted in several images of the aircraft that struck the South Tower of the World Trade Center on 9/11 are real physical objects and not aberrations of the light. The report also notes that commercial Boeing 767-300 aircraft do not have such attachments. This leads to the obvious conclusion that the aircraft that stuck the South Tower of the World Trade Center on 9/11 was not a commercial airliner.

I did not ask the lady that I met at the abovementioned meeting to show me any official identification but I recognized her immediately we first met in the foyer of the Hotel Universal from a photograph of a blonde-haired woman contained in the top left-hand section of the second page of a website article contained at this address:
http://www.goyadiscovery.com/images/COVER_GOYA.pdf.

The juxtaposition of this picture to the content of the accompanying article suggests that this is a photograph of Amparo Sacristian Carrasco. Two of my other travelling companions who were with me in the foyer of the hotel when I met this lady also agreed that the woman I met was the same person shown in this article. The signature my interlocutor wrote on the Spanish language version of the abovementioned report reads "A. Sacristian". I first contacted this lady via her LinkedIn network page under the name of Amparo Sacristian Carrasco. As a result, I have no reason to doubt that the lady I met in Barcelona was anyone other than Amparo Sacristian Carrasco."

Appendix 5 - Updated Summary of my 9/11 Research

In my "9/11 Research Report – An Australian Perspective" of 2010 and my "Why I believe that the Official Narrative on 9/11 is suspect" paper of 2012, I essentially expressed the following conclusions about the events that took place in New York City and in Washington D.C. on 11th September 2001 (known colloquially as "the 9/11 terrorist attacks" or more simply as "911" or "9/11". I personally prefer the term "the 9/11 event" for reasons that will hopefully become clear below:

The official version of the events of 9/11 by the United States Government (USG), and particularly its key agents in the matter, the Fire and Emergency Management Authority (FEMA), the National Institute for Standards and Technology (NIST) and the 9/11 Commission, are, at least, inadequate, if not a complete whitewash. They are simply incredible – that is, not believable.

An alternative hypothesis that the collapse of World Trade Center buildings number one, two and seven (WTC1), (WTC 2) and (WTC 7) was due to a controlled demolition is at least as credible as the official explanation for their collapse which proposes the "Progressive Column Failure (PCF)" hypothesis as the main cause – in fact more so in the light of the evidence now available in the public domain, some of which is cited below. So, the "Controlled Demolition" hypothesis should be more formally and more thoroughly investigated as a serious scientific hypothesis by academic and professional researchers.

The best that can currently be said about the 9/11 event is

that it is an unsolved mass murder. The main reason that it has not yet been solved is, I believe, because the USG refuses to conduct a proper criminal investigation into the crime.

My reasons for arriving at these conclusions are set out below. [Sorry about the repetition but I have embellished the 2010 text so much that without quoting the full text of this version it would not make sense if I truncated it. Perhaps you can speed read the familiar bits].

In the almost twelve years that I have been researching the 9/11 event I have come to regard the following facts as being "reasonably certain" (or, if you like, in legal terms, "proven beyond reasonable doubt"):

1. The official 9/11 narrative as proclaimed by the USG is false because:

    a. There is no plausible scientific reason why the aircraft impacts between the 92nd to 98th and 78th to 84th floors of the North Tower and South Tower respectively of the World Trade Center should have caused both towers to collapse <u>all the way to the ground</u>. Peer reviewed scientific papers by Szuladzinski et al and by Korol et al demonstrate that the "PCF mode" hypothesis, which forms an integral part of the official USG 9/11 narrative, is implausible.[112] It should be

---

[112] See Szuladzinski, G, Szamboti, A, and Johns, R, *Some Misunderstandings Related to WTC Collapse Analysis*, International Journal of Protective Structures, Volume 4, Number 2, 2013, pp117-126 for a persuasive discussion in which they cite three "fatal mistakes" in the Bažantt et al paper (see note 2 below) which supports the official version of why the North Tower collapsed. See also Korol, R.M., Sivakumaran K.S. and Greening, F.R., *Collapse Time Analysis of Multi-Story Structural Steel Buildings*, The Open Civil Engineering Journal, 2011, 5, 25-35 and Korol, R.M. and Sivakumaran K.S., *Reassessing the Plastic Hinge*

noted that NIST's investigations of the collapse of WTC1 and WTC2, the twin towers, did not address the reasons for the collapse of the floors below the point of impact of the aircraft which struck the buildings. It only examined the sequence of events that occurred between the time of impact of the aircraft and the "initiation of collapse". The actual PCF hypothesis was first proposed by Bažant et al[113] in a paper written just a few days after 9/11 which NIST only refers to in a paragraph in its final report (NIST NCSTAR 1-6 at page 323). Of this, NIST says:

"The study performed by Northwestern University (Bažant 2002) was a simplified approximate analysis of the overall collapse … [It] did not address impact damage, fire dynamics, or structural response of the towers. Rather a generalized condition was assumed". But NIST then went on to say that it "agrees with the assessment"[114]. So, the NIST report does not provide a full explanation of why the twin towers collapsed all the way to the ground – it merely accepts Bažant's explanation of why it did and the two abovementioned peer-reviewed

---

Model for Energy Dissipation of Axially Loaded Columns, Journal of Structures, Volume 2014 (2014), Article ID 795257, 7 pages for a report on their physical experiments on the buckling of metal columns subjected to axial loading and a discussion of the more generalized engineering principals involved.

[113] Bažant, Z. and Zhou, Y., "Why did the World Trade Center collapse?- simple analysis," *Journal of Engineering Mechanics*, vol. 128, no. 1, pp. 2–6, 2002, Addendum to *Journal of Engineering Mechanics*, vol. 128, no. 3, pp. 369–370, 2002.

[114] Available at http://fire.nist.gov/bfrlpubs/build05/PDF/b05040.pdf Extracted 21st December 2016.

scientific papers persuasively contest Bažant's conclusions.

b. There is no plausible reason why WTC7 should have collapsed as a result of the office fires allegedly started by falling debris from WTC1 (the North Tower). No steel framed high-rise building had ever collapsed completely due to fire before 9/11 and none has done so since. At the *Justice in Focus 9/11* conference in New York City on 10th September 2016,[115] Professor Leroy Hulsey from the University of Alaska, Fairbanks, presented his preliminary findings into what <u>did not</u> cause WTC7 to collapse. He did so with the accompaniment of a power-point presentation which ended with a slide asking: "Did WTC7 collapse from fire?" The slide then immediately answered this question with a simple word: "No". This is in direct contradiction of the NIST report of November 2008 entitled "Final Report on the Collapse of World Trade Center Building 7"[116] the abstract of which summaries NIST's findings with the words: "This report describes how the fires caused by the debris from the collapse of WTC1 (the north tower) led to the collapse of WTC7". So NIST says that WTC7 "probably" [see point c. below] collapsed due to fire. Hulsey definitively says: "No, it didn't."

---

[115] I attended this conference as an audience participant.
[116] Available at
http://ws680.nist.gov/publication/get_pdf.cfm?pub_id=861610.

c. Video footage, from several different angles, of the collapse of WTC7 shows that this building collapsed symmetrically so all of the support structures right around the building must have failed at approximately the same time and not in the sequential manner suggested in the PCF explanation provided by NIST. NIST's abovementioned report says that it "performed computer simulations of the behaviour of WTC7 on September 11, 2001; and combined the knowledge gained into a probable collapse sequence". NIST graphical presentations of its simulations shows significant deformations of the building structure[117] which are totally absent in the video records of the actual collapse. Moreover, NIST has refused to provide a large portion of its modelling data that was used to perform its simulations on the grounds that to do so "might jeopardize public safety". NIST's explanation as to why and how this building collapsed is therefore incomplete, suspect and hence implausible.

d. Over 150 eye witnesses to the events of 9/11 in New York City reported hearing "explosions" or "bombs" exploding before and during the collapse of all three buildings. Video footage also shows on-site journalists reporting on these events flinching and ducking at the sound of explosions clearly heard in the background of their broadcast locations even before the buildings started to fall. Video footage of New York fire fighters

---

[117] See Figure 3 in the brochure entitled "Fifteen Years Later: On the Physics of High Rise Building Collapses" by Steven Jones, Robert Korol, Anthony Szamboti and Ted Walter available at http://www.europhysicsnews.org/articles/epn/pdf/2016/04/epn201647 4p21.pdf. I met Anthony Szamboti at the Justice in Focus 9/11 conference referred to in this paper.

clearly shows them explaining the sight and sound of sequential explosions as they watched the buildings falling. Explosions were clearly involved in the collapse of all three buildings yet NIST says it did not look for any signs of explosives being used because it says that there was no evidence to suggest that they were. Clearly, NIST ignored large amounts of evidence pertaining to this event because that evidence contradicted its <u>preconceived</u> conclusions about what caused the collapse.[118]

e. A scientific paper by Harrit, Jones et al reported finding traces of unreacted nano-thermite residues in four dust samples collected from Lower Manhattan in the hours and days after 9/11. This paper provides scientific proof that explosives were involved in 9/11. I have met personally with Professor Harrit and another co-author, Australian chemist Dr Frank Legge, to verify their credentials and the veracity of their paper[119]. Their paper provides valid scientific proof that explosives were used in the destruction of the WTC buildings.

---

[118] Professor Graeme MacQueen from the University of Toronto has reviewed over 11,000 pages of eye-witness testimony from those present in New York City on 9/11 and reports the abovementioned findings. He is featured in the DVD "9/11 in the Academic Community", a documentary by Canadian film maker Adnan Zuberi, which exhorts academics around the world to conduct more rigorous research into the 9/11 event particularly addressing the question "What actually happened?" I have exchanged e-mails on several occasions with both Professor MacQueen and Mr Zuberi and have satisfied myself as to their credentials, professionalism and sincerity and I subsequently met Professor McQueen on 8th September 2016 at a film festival in Oakland, California.

[119] Harrit, Niels H., Farrer, Jeffrey, Jones, Steven E., Ryan, Kevin R., Legge, Frank M., Farnsworth, Daniel, Roberts, Greg, Gourley, James R. and Larsen, Bradley R., *Active Thematic Material Discovered in Dust from the 9/11 World Trade Centre Catastrophe*, The Open Chemical Physics Journal, 2009, 2, 7-31.

f. Seismic survey data from the Lamont-Doherty Earth Observatory of Columbia University, in Palisades, N.Y, a seismic observatory some thirty-four miles away from the World Trade Centre, shows that ground disturbances originating from the 9/11 events in New York, and which were initially explained as depicting aircraft impacts and falling debris, have now been reinterpreted by Rousseau so as to demonstrate that the nature of the waves, their velocities, frequencies, and magnitudes invalidate these officially adopted explanations.[120]. This reinterpretation constitutes further scientific evidence which contradicts the official story about 9/11.

g. If explosives were involved in the destruction of WTC1, WTC2 and WTC7 then someone must have had access to those three buildings prior to 9/11 to place those explosive charges. Significant maintenance and upgrade activity is known to have been undertaken in the Twin Towers in the months prior to 9/11 with the full authority of the owner of the Twin Towers, the Port Authority of New York and New Jersey, and head leasee of those two buildings, and owner of WTC7, New York businessman Larry Silverstein.[121]

h. It is unreasonable to assume that Al Qaida or any other Islamic terrorist organization could have gained access to all three buildings to place demolition charges without

---

[120] Source:
http://www.journalof9/11studies.com/resources/RousseauVol34November2012.pdf. Extracted: 2nd September, 2014.

[121] Details of these renovation and maintenance activities can be found in Ryan, Kevin R., "Demolition access to the World Trade Center towers", a four part expose commencing at
http://9/11review.com/articles/ryan/demolition_access_DonPaul.html. Extracted: 27th July, 2010.

being detected, particularly in WTC7 which contained the New York offices of the CIA, the Department of Defense and the Securities and Exchange Commission. Therefore, whoever placed such charges (if the Controlled Demolition hypothesis can be credibly sustained – and some commentators referred to above and below believe that it already has been) must have had assistance from someone with unfettered and unquestioned access to all three buildings – someone sufficiently credible to all who saw them so as not to challenge them or query what they were doing.

i. None of the airliners involved in 9/11 was intercepted after they were reported as being hijacked even though under normal procedures there would have been ample time for them to do so. Air Force jets were scrambled dozens of times earlier that year to intercept troubled or suspected aircraft. Why did they fail to do so on 11th September 2001? Maybe because:

   i.   Intercept procedures were changed a few months before that day.

   ii. Multiple exercises were taking place on 9/11 – many more than usual.

   iii. An extraordinary number of available US Air Force interceptors had been redeployed to northern and western locations, away from the north east sector, to participate in these exercises.

   iv. Radar imagery on 9/11 was confused by the injection of dummy signals into live radar monitors as part of those exercises.

   v.   There was a disruption of the military chain of command on 9/11 with an inexperienced officer being placed in command whilst his superior absented himself from his post. The latter was never disciplined for this breach of duty. Rather, he was promoted.

      None of these unusual Air Force manoeuvres could have been arranged by Islamic terrorists. Much of the detail of these manoeuvres is reported in Michael C. Ruppert's book *"Crossing the Rubicon"*.[122]

j.   A scientific paper by Professor Amparo Sacristan Carrasco, an acknowledged expert on image analysis, reports that the apparent cylindrical shapes shown in photographs of the aircraft that struck the South Tower (WTC2) were real physical objects and not aberrations of the light. Boeing 767-300 commercial aircraft have no such attachments. This leads to the obvious conclusion that the aircraft that struck the South Tower was NOT a commercial airliner. This evidence also constitutes scientific evidence that the official story is wrong. I have met personally with Professor Carrasco to confirm her credentials and the veracity of her paper[123]. She also signed a copy of her paper in my presence as evidence of its authenticity and I now have a copy of that signed document in my possession. In addition, whilst at the *Justice in Focus*

---

[122] *Op cit*, New Society Publishers, Gabriola Island, 2004.
[123] Source: http://www.amics21.com/9/11/report.html. Extracted 10th January 2011.

9/11 conference in New York on 11th September, 2016, Mr William Jacoby, secretary of the newly launched 9/11 Truth Action Project told me that he knew of an eye witness to the impact of this aircraft into the South Tower who reports that the aircraft she saw hit the building was not a commercial airliner. She said that the aircraft that she saw was all grey, with no identifying markings on it and had no windows along its side. As result, I believe that Professor Carrasco's evidence provides independent corroborating evidence to this eye-witness's testimony.

k. The co-chairs of the 9/11 Commission complained that the resources they were provided with to carry out their inquiry were inadequate to do the job and that they were given too little time. They expressed the view that they had been "set up to fail". They also complained that their efforts had been hampered by members of the Bush Administration, the CIA and the Department of Defense.

These are the main arguments that form the basis of my abovementioned conclusions about the 9/11 event but there are many, many, more, dozens in fact, of anomalies, inconsistencies, irregularities and misinterpretations that could be added to the above list which, even if they do not rate as "reasonable certainties" as described above, could justifiably being listed under the headings of "unanswered questions" or "unsatisfactory answers". American writer David Ray Griffin has listed over one hundred such additional facts which could be so classified. His paper *"The 9/11 Commission Report: A 571-*

Page Lie" summarizes his findings.[124] The 9/11 Consensus Panel lists over 40 points which its review panel considers to be "best evidence" that the official narrative on 9/11 cannot be true[125].

2. As a result of the above I believe that we cannot rely upon the current U.S. Government propounded narrative on 9/11 as being a credible explanation of what happened on that day. A fresh inquiry is clearly needed.

3. The contents of the press release covering the *Justice in Focus 9/11* conference noted above are worth considering here[126]. Some of its more insightful comments include:

> "We had the unprecedented opportunity to present before this esteemed panel of legal professionals the forensic evidence that three WTC skyscrapers, WTC 1 and 2 – and WTC 7 not hit by any plane – all featured the key signatures of controlled demolition," said Architects & Engineers for 9/11 Truth founder and president Richard Gage, AIA.
>
> "As Arthur Conan Doyle famously said, 'Once you've eliminated the impossible, whatever remains, however improbable, must be the truth,' said Lawyers Committee for 9/11 Inquiry Vice President Mick Harrison," and "<u>the evidentiary presentations established these forensic facts beyond any reasonable doubt.</u>" (My underlining - Note that it is a group of eminent lawyers that is expressing this opinion.)

---

[124] Source: http://www.911truth.org/article.php?story=20050523112738404. Extracted: 10th August 2010.

[125] See http://www.consensus911.org/the-9-11-consensus-points/ for a list of these points.

[126] The full two-day program and access to the archived videos are at www.911justiceinfocus.org and www.noliesradio.org.

"And how did the official authorities deal with all of this [physical and eyewitness] evidence of controlled demolitions?" asked Professor Emeritus Graeme MacQueen, a member of the 9/11 Consensus Panel and co-editor of the Journal of 9/11 Studies. "The answer is simple. They didn't ... All my studies of the eyewitness testimonies conclude that explosions [independent of plane impacts and resulting fires] *brought down these buildings."*

"The September 11th attacks are one of those high crimes that can cause the very foundations of the law to tremble," said renowned public interest attorney Daniel Sheehan.

4. The upshot of this New York conference is that its final event was the calling of an impromptu board meeting of the Lawyers' Committee for 9/11 Inquiry on the same stage where Abraham Lincoln delivered his famous Cooper Union Address in which the board members, there being an adequate quorum present, passed a resolution to proceed with compiling an application to a US Federal court of appropriate jurisdiction and also the courts of appropriate jurisdiction in the states of New York and New Jersey to convene a Grand Jury in each or any of these jurisdictions to conduct a new investigation into the events of 9/11. The committee is firmly of the opinion, both legally and historically, that those inquiries that have been conducted since the tragic 9/11 event have been woefully inadequate and that no proper criminal investigation has ever been carried out into what is undoubtedly an unsolved mass murder. The committee has also concluded, based on the evidence now available, that the current official US Government sanctioned conspiracy theory of the events of

9/11 cannot possibly be true and that the evidence of its falsehood is overwhelming.

5. It should be noted that it was not just Americans who died on 9/11. Ten Australian citizens were amongst the victims of this crime. So, this is not just an American problem. It is our problem too.

6. Greens candidate for the 2016 U.S. Presidential Election, Jill Stein, on 9th September, 2016, called for a new investigation into 9/11 saying:

> "Led by the families of those who died on 9/11, the American people wanted – and deserved – a comprehensive and independent inquiry into the attacks. The Bush administration initially said an inquiry was unnecessary, claiming that the perpetrators had been identified and their methods and motives were clear.
>
> It is well known that the 9/11 Commission produced a report containing so many omissions and distortions that *Harper's Magazine* described it as 'whitewash as public service; – a document that 'defrauds the nation.' The co-chairs of the 9/11 Commission wrote a book just two years after the final commission report, saying, 'We were set up to fail.' The 9/11 Commission was not given enough money, time, or access to relevant classified information" and

7. "The families and friends of those who were murdered on 9/11 deserve justice ... they also deserve to know the truth."[127]

---

[127] See http://www.theblaze.com/stories/2016/09/10/jill-stein-calls-for-new-investigation-to-find-the-truth-about-9/11/

The main reasons I am so concerned about the way our response to 9/11 has unfolded is because of the danger it poses to the core values that we profess to believe in. We profess to believe in personal freedom, democratic government, rule of law and human rights. How can we continue to maintain and pursue these core values if we allow nearly three thousand people to be murdered in broad daylight with the whole world watching but then ignore large swathes of evidence pertinent to the event and avoid conducting a proper criminal investigation into the crime? If we continue to do so then we are allowing the true perpetrators of this crime to get away with murder. And if we allow that to happen how can any of us have any confidence that we are safe and protected by the political, judicial, legal and military institutions that we have established and maintain to secure our lives, liberty, property and the pursuit of a happy and fulfilling life for ourselves and our loved ones? All of the core values noted above are at risk if we do not deliver justice to those who have suffered as a result of this crime.

Appendix 6 - My attempts to speak Truth to Power in Australia with respect to the 9/11 Event

Over the past decade I have attempted to bring to the attention of the Australian Government and the Australia people generally the fact that there is substantial and persuasive evidence now available in the public domain that proves beyond reasonable doubt that the official United States Government's account of what happened in New York City and Washington D.C. on 11th September 2001(commonly known as 9/11) cannot possibly be true. In the main, my attempts to do so have been unsuccessful.

Laid out below are examples of my most recent attempt to bring to the attention of Australia's political leaders facts, not theories, that are now readily available to anyone who cares to look, that 9/11 was "an inside job". These facts are detailed in two current lawsuits that are currently before the American courts together with a newly published report from the University of Alaska Fairbanks which proves that World Trade Center building number 7 (WTC7) was brought down by a controlled demolition. Since it takes weeks, if not months, to rig a building for controlled demolition, this report alone proves that 9/11 must have been pre-planned by people with unfettered access to that building.

The response of the Australian Government to my advices has been to, firstly, ignore them, and then, subsequently, to censor my reports to them.

The particular vehicle that I chose to convey my latest set of advices to the Australian Government was the requirements of the recently passed Foreign Influence Transparency Scheme [FITS] Act 2018, which, by coincidence, required that an organization for which I was the Australian spokesperson, Truth Outreach Inc. doing business as 9/11 Truth Action Project (9/11TAP), met the definition of a "foreign political organization" as defined by that act. The act required me to report all of my outreach activities in my capacity as spokesperson for 9/11TAP to the Australian Government in the proscribed manner.

The emails cited below provide evidence of the attempt by the Australian Government to censor my communications to them on this matter. Although somewhat repetitious, they do show the diversity of my attempts to convey this information to both the media and the government. I have quoted them in full. I think you will understand why when you have read the full essay.

Text of an Email sent to Australian Politicians on 4th September 2019

"Greetings all,

I bring to your attention the draft final report of the study into the collapse of WTC7, the third building to collapse in New York City on 9/11, by Professor Leroy Hulsey of the University of Alaska Fairbanks which is available for download here:

https://www.ae9/11truth.org/wtc7.

The study entailed the construction of a detail computer simulation constructed from the construction drawings of the building for the entire building and subjected to vigorous testing and verification. On page 111 of the report, Professor Hulsey concludes that:

"The simultaneous failure of all core columns over 8 stories followed 1.3 seconds later by the simultaneous failure of all exterior columns over 8 stories produces almost exactly the behavior observed in videos of the collapse. The collapse could have started at various floors starting at Floor 16 and below and produced the same behavior.

It is our conclusion that the collapse of WTC 7 was a global failure involving the near simultaneous failure of all columns in the building and not a progressive collapse involving the sequential failure of columns throughout the building."

The US$300,000 four-year study was commissioned by Architects and Engineers for 9/11 Truth (AE9/11Truth), a section 501(c)(3) non-profit organization which has 3,131 architects and engineers who have called for a new investigation into the collapse of all three buildings on 9/11, the Twin Towers of the World Trade Center (WTC1 & 2) and the 47-story WTC7, which was not hit by an aeroplane, but which collapsed straight down into its own footprint eight hours after the collapse of the Twin Towers.

The report directly contradicts the report on the collapse of WTC7 by the National Institute of Standards and Technology (NIST) which was the official US Government agency tasked with explaining why the building fell down. NIST acknowledges that their explanation that office fires alone caused the collapse would have been the first time in history that a steel framed high-rise building collapsed solely due to fire. NIST proposed the progressive collapse hypothesis as the basis of its conclusions which Hulsey's study specifically disproves.

AE9/11Truth has expressed the view that the only way that they are aware of that such a collapse can occur is by the use of demolition charges. According to AE9/11Truth, no other plausible explanation is possible.

Since it takes months to prepared a building for demolition, for WTC7 to have collapsed just hours after the initial aircraft impacts, then the collapse must have been planned and prepared long before 9/11 occurred, by people who had unfettered access to the building in the weeks and months prior to 9/11.

In other words, Professor Hulsey's report PROVES that 9/11 was an 'INSIDE JOB'. This is NOT a 'crazy conspiracy theory'. This is now PROVEN SCIENTIFIC FACT.

Sincerely.

David F. Palmer."

Advices by persons who are required to register with the Foreign Influence Transparency Scheme (FITS) are called "registrations".

Text of a FITS Registration by me on 9th September 2019

"Commenced distribution of a flyer that reports the release of a report on 3rd September 2019 by Professor Leroy Hulsey from the University of Alaska Fairbanks which proves that World Trade Center Building number 7 was demolished by explosives on 11th September 2001. WTC7, which was directly across the street from the North Tower of the World Trade Center, was not hit by an airplane but it collapsed straight down into its own footprint eight hours after the twin towers collapsed. Professor Hulsey's report PROVES 9/11 was an INSIDE JOB."

The text of that flyer read as follows:

"WTC7 Simulation Disproves NIST Report

A draft final report of the study into the collapse of WTC7, the third building to collapse in New York City on 9/11, by Professor Leroy Hulsey of the University of Alaska Fairbanks, was released on 3rd September 2019. A copy of the report is available for download here: https://www.ae9/11truth.org/wtc7.

The study entailed the construction of a detail computer simulation developed from the construction drawings of the building, for the entire building, and was subjected to vigorous testing and verification. On page 111 of the report, Professor Hulsey concludes that:

"The simultaneous failure of all core columns over 8 stories followed 1.3 seconds later by the simultaneous failure of all exterior columns over 8 stories produces almost exactly the behavior observed in videos of the collapse ... ...

It is our conclusion that the collapse of WTC 7 was a global failure involving the near simultaneous failure of all columns in the building and not a progressive collapse involving the sequential failure of columns throughout the building."

The US$300,000 four-year study was commissioned by Architects and Engineers for 9/11 Truth (AE9/11Truth), a section 501(c)(3) non-profit organization which has 3,131 architects and engineers who have called for a new investigation into the collapse of all three buildings on 9/11, the Twin Towers of the World Trade Center (WTC1 & 2) and the 47-story WTC building number 7. WTC7, which was not hit by an airplane, collapsed straight down into its own footprint eight hours after the collapse of the Twin Towers just like a Controlled Demolition.

The report directly contradicts the report on the collapse of WTC7 by the National Institute of Standards and Technology (NIST) which was the official US Government agency tasked with explaining why the building fell down. NIST acknowledges that their explanation that office fires alone caused the collapse would have been the first time in history that a steel-framed high-raise building collapsed solely due to fire. NIST proposed the progressive collapse hypothesis as the basis of its conclusions which Hulsey's study now specifically disproves.

AE9/11Truth has expressed the view that the only way that they are aware of that such a collapse can occur is by the use of demolition charges. According to AE9/11Truth, no other plausible explanation is possible.

> *Since it takes months to prepare a building for demolition, for WTC7 to have collapsed just hours after the initial aircraft impacts, then the collapse must have been planned and prepared long before 9/11 occurred, by people who had unfettered access to the building in the weeks and months prior to 9/11. In other words, Professor Hulsey's report PROVES that 9/11 was an INSIDE JOB [underlining in the original].*
>
> *This is NOT a 'crazy conspiracy theory'. This is now PROVEN SCIENTIFIC FACT [underlining in the original].*
>
> *This material is communicated by David Frank Palmer on behalf of Truth Outreach Inc. AKA 9/11 Truth Action Project. This disclosure is made under the Foreign Influence Transparency Scheme Act 2018"*

[This last sentence was a legal requirement under the FITS act]."

During this same period, I also distributed a flyer summarizing the two American court cases I had been reporting on, formatted as a two column, one-sided, A4 piece of paper to enable it to be pinned to notice boards. That flyer read as follows:

"Flyer re US Court Cases

U.S. Attorney in New York to Convene a Grand Jury to Consider Evidence that the World Trade Center Buildings Were Destroyed by Explosives

Petitions filed on April 10, 2018, 30th July 2018 and 12th March 2019 by the **Lawyers' Committee for 9/11 Inquiry** to the U.S. Attorney for the Southern District of New York present evidence that has been assembled by Architects and Engineers for 9/11 Truth in the last several years showing that explosives were used to take down three (yes, three!) buildings in New York City on 9/11/2001 and requesting that a grand jury be convened to consider this evidence.

The petitions with their 60 exhibits and supplementary information can be read at https://www.lawyerscommitteefor9-11inquiry.org/ via the "Grand Jury Petition" link at the top of the page.

A response dated November 7, 2018 sent from U.S. Attorney Geoffrey Berman's office stated that it will comply with the request for a grand jury investigation but it has refused to confirm that it has actually done so. On 6th September 2019 the Lawyers Committee applied to the court for a Writ of Mandamus to order the US Attorney to confirm he has done so or, if not, to now do so.

Legal procedures can be protracted so it could take some time, perhaps years, before the outcome of these initiatives is known but it is important to ensure that they are progressing. Grand juries are held in secret so they will not be open to the public but they are very powerful procedures that have the authority to summons and subpoena anyone they choose. The Lawyers' Committee for 9/11 Inquiry, which is a sister organization with the 9/11 Truth Action Project, is making every effort they can to assist in the grand jury process and to make sure it happens.

For more information or to get involved and show your support, you can visit: www.9/11tap.org, www.lcfor9/11.org, or www.ae9/11truth.org.

Lawyers Committee for 9/11 Inquiry sues the US Department of Justice and the FBI

Lawyers Committee for 9/11 Inquiry filed suit in the District Court for the District of Columbia (case 1-19-cv-00824 filed 03/25/19 Document 1) against the United States Department of Justice and the Federal Bureau of Investigation for failing to comply with a 2014 federal law requiring the FBI, and 2014-15 9/11 Review Commission, to review and evaluate evidence available to it at the time of the Commission's inquiry and to report such evidence to congress. The suit requests the court to issue a Mandamus order for the defendants to now comply. The complaint cites seven classes of information the FBI and the 9/11 Review Commission failed to consider and report, including:

- the use of explosives to demolish WTC buildings 1, 2 and 7;

- the arrest of five individuals, who self-identified as being

Israeli, who later claimed that they were there to observe the event;

- video and photographic evidence collected by the FBI covering the Pentagon attack on that day;

- details of plane debris collected that day which contained serial numbers that could identify the planes they came from;

- apparent financial support to the alleged hijackers from Saudi sources including the Saudi royal family; and

- anomalies in reports of calls from alleged passengers on hijacked airplanes to relatives on the ground on 9/11.

Details available here: https://www.9/11tap.org/557-news-releases/798-fbi-and-department-of-justice-sued-for-failure-to-perform-duties."

Text of an Email from me to National Press Club on 11th September 2019

"Greetings all,

Please be advised that on 11th September 2019 the President of the Lawyers Committee for 9/11 Inquiry (LCfor9/11Inquiry) held a press conference at the National Press Club in Washington DC in which he advised that the Lawyers Committee had lodged with the abovementioned court [the District Court for the Southern District of New York] *a petition requesting the court to order the US Attorney for the Southern District of New York to disclose whether or not he had empanelled a Grand Jury to receive and consider the evidence it had submitted in its petitions of 10th April 2018 and 30th July 2018 (a copy of the latter of which is available here: https://www.lawyerscommitteefor9-11inquiry.org/lc-doj-first-amended-grand-jury-petition/) and, if not, to order the US Attorney to empanel such a Grand Jury. On 7th November 2018 the US Attorney advised that he would comply with the law in respect of this petition but when asked in July 2019 if he had actually done so the US Attorney declined to say so due to the secrecy requirements of Grand Jury processes.*

LCfor9/11Inquiry President, Attorney David Meiswinkle's address to the press conference may be viewed here: https://www.lawyerscommitteefor9-11inquiry.org/. In his press conference address Mr Meiswinkle expressed the legal opinion of the lawyers committee that the evidence of controlled demolition of the Twin Towers of the World Trade Center (WTC1 and 2) and of the Salomon Brother Building (WTC7) on 11th September 2001 by the use of explosives was 'dispositive', a legal term which he explained meant 'beyond doubt'.

Sincerely,

David F. Palmer"

Supplementary to my NPC e-mail on 11th September 2019:

"Sorry folks,

The e-mail below [above as presented here] *should also have carried the disclosure: 'This material is communicated by David Frank Palmer on behalf of Truth Outreach Inc. AKA 9/11 Truth Action Project. This disclosure is made under the Foreign Influence Transparency Scheme Act 2018.'"* [That legal requirement that I have forgot to add to the email].

Text of e-mails from me sent to the National Press Club on 13th September 2019

"Ladies and Gentlemen,

This morning I sent the following e-mail to four Australian senators and three House Representatives and several other private individuals:

'Greetings All,

Please be advised that on 11th September 2019 the President of the Lawyers Committee for 9/11 Inquiry (LCfor9/11Inquiry) held a press conference at the National Press Club in Washington DC in which he advised that the Lawyers Committee had lodged with the abovementioned court [the District Court for the Southern District of New York] *a petition requesting the court to order the US Attorney for the*

Southern District of New York to disclose whether or not he had empaneled a Grand Jury to receive and consider the evidence it had submitted in its petitions of 10th April 2018 and 30th July 2018 (a copy of the latter of which is available here: https://www.lawyerscommitteefor9-11inquiry.org/lc-doj-first-amended-grand-jury-petition/) and, if not, to order the US Attorney to empanel such a Grand Jury. On 7th November 2018 the US Attorney advised that he would comply with the law in respect of this petition but when asked in July 2019 if he had actually done so the US Attorney declined to say so due to the secrecy requirements of Grand Jury processes.

LCfor9/11Inquiry President Attorney David Meiswinkle's address to the press conference may be viewed here: https://www.lawyerscommitteefor9-11inquiry.org/. In his press conference address Mr. Meiswinkle expressed the legal opinion of the lawyers committee that the evidence of controlled demolition of the Twin Towers of the World Trade Center (WTC1 and 2) and of the Salomon Brother Building (WTC7) on 11th September 2001 by the use of explosives was 'dispositive', a legal term which he explained meant 'beyond doubt'.

Sincerely,

David F. Palmer

This material is communicated by David Frank Palmer on behalf of Truth Outreach Inc. AKA 9/11 Truth Action Project. This disclosure is made under the Foreign Influence Transparency Scheme Act 2018.

In addition, I have recently distributed the attached flyer [attached to the email, that is. The flyer reported the evidence cited above] *to several university campuses in Perth. It reports the finding of a four-year US$300,000 study by Professor Leroy Hulsey of the University of Alaska Fairbanks which concludes that for World Trade Center building number 7, WTC7, to have collapsed in the manner in which multiple video recordings show it collapsing could only have occurred if ALL of the support columns holding up the building failed at the same time over eight floors of the building (or, within 1.3 seconds of each other according to Hulsey's report). The non-profit organization Architects and Engineers for 9/11 Truth Inc., AE9/11Truth, which has collected the signatures of over 3,000 architects and engineers calling for a new investigation in 9/11, states categorically that the only way that they are aware of that this could happen is by the use of demolition charges.*

The evidence that the official US Government's explanation as to what happened in New York City on the 11th September 2001 cannot possibly be true is overwhelming. Or, to use the phraseology of the above quoted American Attorney, David Meiswinkle, the evidence that the three steel-framed high-rise buildings that collapsed in New York on that day were demolished by the use of explosives is 'dispositive', or 'beyond doubt'.

Isn't it about time that Australian journalists grew a backbone and started reporting the truth of this event instead of perpetually regurgitating the total and utter bovine manure that the United States Government, and its lackey, the Australian Government, have been peddling these past eighteen years?

Sincerely,

David F. Palmer'

This material is communicated by David Frank Palmer on behalf of Truth Outreach Inc. AKA 9/11 Truth Action Project. This disclosure is made under the Foreign Influence Transparency Scheme Act 2018."

Text of e-mails from me sent to the National Press Club on 14th September 2019

"Ladies and Gentlemen,

Following my email below ['below' refers to the email of 13th September as cited above here], *can I direct your attention to the 1.38-minute video clip available at this site (shown by Alaska TV station KTVA):* https://www.ktva.com/story/41015153/fire-did-not-cause-world-trade-center-building-7-collapse-uaf-study-suggests

Could you not at least report this?

Cheers.

David Palmer.

This material is communicated by David Frank Palmer on behalf of Truth Outreach Inc. AKA 9/11 Truth Action Project. This disclosure is made under the Foreign Influence Transparency Scheme Act 2018."

Text of an e-mail from me sent to Media Watch on 14th September 2019.

"I sent an e-mail to the National Press Club this morning which says: "can I direct your attention to the 1.38-minute video clip available at this site (shown by Alaska TV station KTVA):

https://www.ktva.com/story/41015153/fire-did-not-cause-world-trade-center-building-7-collapse-uaf-study-suggests.

Could you not at least report this?"

In a previous e-mail to them said, inter alia: "Attorney David Meiswinkle's address to the press conference [at NPC Washington] may be viewed here: https://www.lawyerscommitteefor9-11inquiry.org/" which reports the same event.

Could you please incorporate this information in your next Media Watch broadcast? Come back to me if you need any further information or a full copy of the two e-mails I sent to them earlier.

This material is communicated by David Frank Palmer on behalf of Truth Outreach Inc. AKA 9/11 Truth Action Project. This disclosure is made under the Foreign Influence Transparency Scheme Act 2018."

Appendix 7 – The Global Financial Elite

"Who are Global Financial Elite and what are the crimes they are alleged to have committed?

It is not uncommon these days for social justice commentators to refer to the "Global Financial Elite" or just the "Global Elite" in ways that are not particularly complimentary.

Who are these "elite" people?

Some clues as to their actual identity may be gained from some of the sources summarized below.

The image immediately below is one example that purports to explain the global governance structure[128], which is attributed to "one Fritz Springmeier, an author and educator who has devoted his career to exposing Illuminati connections and history"[129]

---

[128] See this website: 13 Powerful Families In The World That Apparently Control Everything; https://www.indiatimes.com/culture/who-we-are/these-are-the-13-families-in-the-world-that-apparently-control-everything-from-politics-to-terrorism-257642.html

[129] See: 13 Bloodlines | Illuminati Families Controlling the Cabal; https://www.ranker.com/list/main-families-of-illuminati/mike-rothschild)

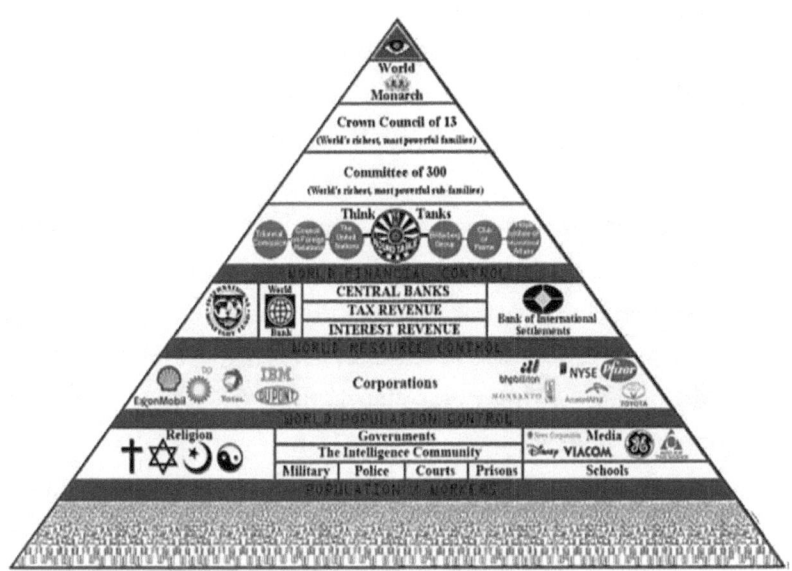

Atop the image is the "all seeing eye", a symbol usually associated with the Freemason's organization.

The "World Monarch" is not specified in the above image but presumably it is the current patriarch or matriarch of the most prominent of the 13 families, not necessarily European royalty, and may be even one of the more recent additions to that class.[130]

The Crown Council of 13 is Springmeier's 13 Illuminati families of which a CIA website contains more details. [131]

The Committee of 300 is described in detail in Dr John Coleman's book *The Conspirators Hierarchy: The Committee of 300, 4th Edition*[132]. The work also traces the instruments of Global Elite dominance going back to Rev Thomas Malthust of the

---

[130] It has been suggested that Bill Gates is such a person.
[131] https://www.cia.gov/library/abbottabad-compound/FC/FC2F5371043C48FDD95AEDE7B8A49624_Springmeier.-.Bloodlines.of.the.Illuminati.R.pdf.
[132] Ibid, World in Review, Carson City, NV, USA: 2006.

"too many people consuming too few natural resources" fame and the British East India Company, the world's first real multinational corporation, which was founded in 1600AD. The work also introduces the birth of Eugenics and the concept of the "Useless Eaters".

This author cannot vouch for the authority of this particular presentation and some of it may constitute little more than fiction, speculation or just an absurd conspiracy theory, although the above "Council of 13" includes many of the entities listed below. Moreover, Springmeier claims that the listed 13 families are practicing "Satan" worshipers. This author doubts that accusation. Some, particularly the founders of these financial dynasties, may have worshiped Mammon[133] but this writer doubts they actually worshiped Satan.

To your humble scribe, they are just very wealthy families who may have accumulated their wealth either by nefarious means or through the application of spectacular and talented business acumen, or perhaps a skillful combination of both. Their founders were, after all, exceptional people. Many elite lists are decades, even centuries, old and the above references give no indication whether those family fortunes are still intact or whether they have been frittered away by indolent and extravagant descendants.

A more recent assessment may be the cohort of wealthy individuals who American writer David Rothkopf refers as the "Superclass", which he speculates approximate 4,000/5,000 individuals (about half of the 1% of the 1% of the 1%, so to speak).[134]

---

[133] See the King James Bible, Mathew 6, verses 19-21 and 24 for an authoritative reference of that term.
[134] See: Rothkopf, David; *Superclass, The Global Power Elite and the World they are making*; Farrar, Straus and Giroux; New York; 2008).

Rothkopf does not name names but Springmeier has suggested, in his list of 13 "Illuminati" families, that they comprise the Houses of Rothschild, Rockefeller, Astor, Bundy, Collins, DuPont, Freeman, Kennedy, Li, Onassis, Russell, Van Duyn, and the descendants of Merovingian dynasty of Middle-Ages France. He later added the Houses of Krupp and Disney to his list of Illuminati bloodlines.

To this, one might add the Houses of Windsor, Orange, Morgan, Vanderbilt, Schiff, Lazard, Ford, Carnegie and Ziff. To this extended list one might further add the newest well-known members of this "super" class: Messrs Gates, Bezos, Zuckerberg, Musk, Branson and the House of Saud. The media moguls should probably also be included and the most well-known of those would be the Murdoch and Hearst families[135].

At the risk of sounding anti-Semitic, it might also be noted that the elite cohort of Global Jewry (but not all people of the Jewish faith) is disproportionately featured among the Global Elite, particularly those prominent in world banking industry. For example, just eight families, four of which reside in the US, have 80% ownership of the New York Federal Reserve Bank, the largest and most influential of the twelve Federal Reserve banks in the USA. Of the eight, seven; the partners of Goldman Sachs, the Lehmans and the Kuhn Loebs of New York; the Rothschilds of Paris and London; the Warburgs of Hamburg; the Lazards of Paris; and the Israel Moses Seifs of Rome are Jewish. The eighth is the Rockefeller family which in Christian.[136] But for balance, religion-wise, it should also be noted that the House of Saud, cited above and mentioned

---

[135] These additional entities have noted from various sources from the writer's reading over the years but without noting the specific reference at the time.

[136] See: https://www.globalresearch.ca/the-federal-reserve-cartel-the-eight-families/25080.

further below, is Muslim. So, the Global Elite is not necessarily defined by either religion or ethnicity.

The Forbes Global Billionaires list which is published each year might be added to the aforementioned. Those not mentioned previously include the Arnault, Slim Helu, Francoise Bettencourt Meyers, Walton (Jim, Alice), David Thomson, Phil Knight, and Koch (Charles and Julia) families and Messrs Zhao, Buffett, Page, Brin, Ellison, Ballmer, Ambani, Adani, Bloomberg, Ortega, Dell, Zhang Yiming, Schwarz and Zeng plus Mses MacKenzie Scott; and that's just the top thirty on the 2022 list. There are a further 147 whose wealth is recorded as being US$10 billion or greater. The total for 2022 lists is 2,668 individuals and families whose individual wealth exceeds US$1 billion.

Oxfam's January 2023 report entitled *Survival of the Rich* reports that:

- 81 Billionaires hold more wealth than 50% of the world combined, and

- The richest 1% holds 45.6% of global wealth, while the poorest half of the world has just 0.75%.

The Cohort of loyal servants to the Global Elite who American scholar Peter Phillips refers to in his book *Giants: The Global Power Elite*[137] should also be mentioned. In that work, Phillips names the 17 major asset management firms that manage the bulk of equity investments in the world's largest corporations (including their own cross holdings). They are Blackrock, Vanguard, JP Morgan Chase, Allianz SE (PIMCO), UBS, Bank of America Merrill Lynch, Barclays PLC, State Street, Fidelity, Bank of New York Mellon, AXA Group, Capital

---

[137] *Ibid*; Seven Stories Press; New York, Oakland, London; 2018.

Group, Goldman Sachs, Credit Suisse, Prudential, Morgan Stanley and Amondi/Credit Agricole. The work also lists the 199 directors of these firms (including their multiple board appointments). The funds managed by these entities are not their own and their client lists are confidential. No doubt those client lists include many of the names of individuals and families listed above.

The not-for-profit Foundations are also concentrations of wealth but each of these is usually associated with one of the aforementioned Global Elite families, particularly the American ones. These, together with off-shore tax havens, are repositories of family wealthy, still usually controlled by the families, but in a form that renders them free of taxation.

Organizations and institutions that support this privileged group, should probably also be mentioned. They might include: The World Economic Forum, Bilderberg Group, Trilateral Commission, Club of Rome, The Business Roundtable, the Skull and Bones Order and similar consultative and possibly collaborative organizations. Global governance institutions such as the United Nations, World Bank, International Monetary Fund, World Trade Organization, Bank for International Settlements, etc., could also be added.

Other writers in this field have been less individual and family name specific whilst addressing the same essential criterion. Examples include:

- Jones, Alan B.; *How the World Really Works*; ABJ Press, Paradise, Calf; 1996,

- Avant, Finnemore and Sell, Ed's; *Who Governs the Globe?*; Cambridge University Press, Cambridge and other offices; 2010, and

- Domhoff, G. William; *Who Rules America: Challenges to Corporate and Class Dominance*; McGraw Hill Higher Education; New York and others; 2010.

If Rothkopf is approximately right with his 4,000/5,000 estimate of the individuals who comprise the "Superclass", and if the Forbes 2022 billionaire list, with just 2,668 individual listings, captures slightly more than half of that number, then it would appear that many of the members of the Superclass are doing a good job in maintaining their anonymity.

As noted above, the 2,668 individuals cited by Forbes represent just one third of 1% of 1% of 1% of the world's current population of approximately 7.975 billion people.

It is interesting to note that many of the members of the financial Global Elite are, or were, pioneers in new and emerging, for their time, technologies and industries: Vanderbilt for railroads, Carnegie for Steel, Ford for automobiles, Rockefeller and al Saud for oil, and Page, Brin, Gates, Bezos, and Musk for information technologies. Who will it be for Artificial Intelligence, Genetic Engineering and other contemporary emerging technologies?

And as far as the specific identities of some of the families listed above are concerned, it may be that many of the traditional wealthy elite have not been able to maintain the relative status amongst their peers as well as their forebears did. Perhaps their wealth has not grown at the same rate of that of the after-inflation economies generally, perhaps due to poor or ultra-conservative investment management strategies.

And perhaps, as noted above, some may have even squandered the family fortune and slipped from the ranks of the really wealthy. For example, Cornelius Vanderbilt was the richest man in America when he died in 1877 but by the mid-20th century the family had to divest itself of much of its prestigious real estate, as the New York times, in its 24th September 1989 edition, reported in a review of the book by Arthur T. Vanderbilt II, entitled *Fortune's Children: the Fall of the House of Vanderbilt.*

Another example is the House of Rothschild which, although fabulously wealthy in the early nineteenth century, probably the richest in the world at that time, suffered significant declines in its German, Austrian, French and Neapolitan branches as a result of significant anti-Semitic policies of various regimes throughout the later 19th and early 20th centuries. Interestingly, despite one source estimating the Rothschild family's wealth exceeded US$400 billion, it listed what it claims are the two wealthiest individuals within that family are David Meyer Rothschild with a net worth of US10 billion and Lord Jacob Rothschild, the 4th Baron Rothschild, with a net worth of US$5 billion[138]. If that is so, then the family wealth must be spread over hundreds of individuals.

Whether the descendants of the Merovingian dynasty of Middle-Ages France, highlighted by Springmeier, would still make the elite list today is unknown to this writer. This writer also notes that the de Medici family of Florence, which dominated middle-ages Italy and France, also appears to have fallen significantly in financial status. No doubt there are similar falls from prominence.

The Wikipedia has a page on most of these families where more detailed biographies for each are available.

---

[138] See: https://www.thethings.com/richest-living-members-of-rothschild-family-net-worth/#lord-jacob-rothschild-4th-baron-rothschild-has-a-net-worth-of-5-billion.

How much are the Global Elite actually worth financially?

The individuals listed in the Forbes billionaire list are reported to have a collective total net worth of US$14.7 trillion. In the 2022 list, the highest ranking was Elton Musk with a reported wealth of US$219 billion but just one year later that estimate had dropped to US$146.1 billion and the number one spot taken by Bernard Arnault at US$181.6 billion.[139]

Of the families not listed by Forbes, the House of Saud is reputed to be worth US$1.4 trillion spread amongst some 15,000 individuals but with just 2,000 holding most of that family's wealth.[140] For example, the Wikipedia estimates the personal wealth of Crown Prince Mohammed bin Salman's at US$3.0 billion in 2018[141] and that of his father, King Salman is estimated to be worth US$18 billion, so, no doubt the prince's wealth will increase substantially when he inherits the throne. This was the case of the British Crown Prince Charles, whose wealth was estimated at US440 million before he became King Charles III. Upon his mother's death, he inherited some of his Queen Elizabeth II's personal wealth, which the same source estimated as being US$88 billion.

The same source also reported the Kuwaiti, Qatari, Abu Dhabi, Qatari, Thai, Dubai and Brunei royal families being worth US$360 billion, US$253 billion, US$150 billion, US$60 billion, US$28 billion and US$18 billion respectively.[142] With

---

[139] *ibid.*
[140] See: https://www.cnbc.com/2018/08/18/this-royal-familys-wealth-could-be-more-than-1-trillion.html.
[141] See: https://en.wikipedia.org/wiki/Mohammed_bin_Salman.
[142] See: https://www.msn.com/en-au/travel/news/the-shocking-wealth-of-the-world-s-richest-royal-families/ss-AA17H210?ocid=msedgdhp&pc=U531&cvid=27a005f23fcc4ce586b08faf017e7c5c#image=29).

respect to the British royal family, the exact amount that King Charles inherited is unknown since the late queen's will is sealed by law for ninety years after her death. In addition, the prince became trustee of the Crown Estates which is estimated to be worth US$19.5 billion but it is not clear as to whether that is included in the above-mentioned total wealth estimate.[143]

The House of Rothschild is collectively reported to be worth US$450 billion,[144] although this writer has seen estimates higher, as much as US$750 billion.[145] Another source estimates the Rockefeller family's net worth at over US$360 billion.[146]

Within the United States, in July 2018, Business Insider reported the wealth of the top 28 families as:

1. Walton family: Net worth: $169.7 billion

2. Koch family: Net worth: $107 billion

3. Mars family: Net worth: $72 billion

4. Cargill-MacMillan family: Net worth: $38.8 billion

5. (Edward) Johnson family: Net worth: $38.7 billion

6. Cox family: Net worth: $37.2 billion

7. Pritzker family: Net worth: $26.5 billion

8. Duncan family: Net worth: $24.8 billion

---

[143] See: https://www.augustman.com/my/amselect/hit-list/heres-the-net-worth-of-king-charles-iii-and-what-he owns/#:~:text=According%20to%20Fortune%2C%20the%20net%20worth%20of%20King,Things%20Owned%20By%20The%20World%E2%80%99s%20Fourth%20Richest%20Man.

[144] See: https://www.wealthypersons.com/rothschild-family-net-worth-2020-2021/.

[145] Reference not noted at time of reading.

[146] See: https://caknowledge.com/rockefeller-family-net-worth-forbes/#Conclusion_Rockefeller_family_Net_Worth.

9. Hearst family: Net worth: $24.5 billion

10. Lauder family: Net worth: $22.4 billion

11. Newhouse family: Net worth: $18.5 billion

12. SC Johnson family: Net worth: $18.2 billion

13. Dorrance family: Net worth: $17.1 billion

14. Ziff family: Net worth: $14.4 billion

15. du Pont family: Net worth: $14.3 billion

16. Hunt family: Net worth: $13.7 billion

17. Busch family: Net worth: $13.4 billion

18. Bass family: Net worth: $13.3 billion

19. Goldman family: Net worth: $13.2 billion

20. Sackler family: Net worth: $13 billion

21. Brown family: Net worth: $12.3 billion

22. Marshall family: Net worth: $12 billion

23. Mellon family: Net worth: $11.5 billion

24. Stryker family: Net worth: $11.1 billion

Tied 27. Rockefeller (despite the above),

Cathy and Butt families: Net worth: $11 billion

28. Gallo family Net worth: $10.7 billion

[147]

The Bloomberg Billionaires Index of 500 individuals for 2023 lists 199 individuals with assets in excess of US10 billion[148]

---

[147] See: https://www.businessinsider.com/richest-billionaire-families-america-2018-7.
[148] See: https://www.bloomberg.com/billionaires/.

including most of the above but also including the Russian oligarchs and other Chinese, Japanese, Indian and others billionaires elsewhere in the world. Interestingly, the names Rockefeller and Rothschild do not appear in that list.

These estimates may be indicative, but, as the above example of Elton Musk and the Rothschild family shows, wealth estimates tend to vary through time and some estimates vary widely according to source, so there are probably no accurate authoritative estimates of the true wealth of these long-standing and diverse family dynasties, perhaps even by the families themselves. The Rockefeller wealth estimate cited above also states that: "a major portion of Rockefeller net worth is also hidden through third-party fiduciary accounts" and its "wealth also includes over 300 patents and copyrights".[149]

Similar comments could no doubt be made of most major family fortunes since nominees, trusts, off-balance-sheet assets, foundations and offshore tax havens, all of which are perfectly legal, are a common feature of the wealth repositories of the very rich.

It should also be noted that wealth is not the only measure of influence. The Time 100[150] classifies its 2022 list of the world's most influential people into Artists, Innovators, Titans, Leaders, Icons and Pioneers.

Among its contemporary "Leaders" it includes Volymyr Zelensky of Ukraine, Xi Jinping of China, Joe Biden of USA, Ursula von der Leyen of the EU, Vladimir Putin of the Russian Federation[151] and Olaf Scholz of Germany. Its "Titans", whatever that title means, include Oprah Winfrey and Christine Lagarde. Most of the other names on Time's 100 list, however,

---

[149] See: caknowlegde.com; op cit.
[150] See: https://time.com/collection/100-most-influential-people-2022/.
[151] Sometimes contemporaneously described as the richest man in the world today.

are unknown to this writer.[152] It is interesting to note that the Pope and the Dali Lama don't make the list, nor does David Attenborough, Greta Thunberg or Klaus Schwab.[153]

With respect to the last-mentioned well-known contemporary global influencer, Prof Klaus Schwab, and the organization he founded, the World Economy Forum (WEF), the Wikipedia quotes one think tank as saying: *the Forum is planning to replace a recognised democratic model with a model where a self-selected group of 'stakeholders' make decisions on behalf of the people.* The think tank summarises that we are increasingly entering a world where gatherings such as Davos are 'a silent global coup d'état' to capture governance.[154]

Why does all matter anyway?

Because if social justice commentators are going to talk and write about the Global Elite as though they are the people who should be held accountable for the ills of the world, then we really should have some idea as to who we are actually talking about. Not just vague biographical descriptions of some nebulous class of human beings but a comprehensive list of real people complete with their names, addresses and a current photograph.

Where's the evidence of wrongdoing?

As indicated in the introduction, many writers allege that the Global Financial Elite are ruthlessly exploiting the world for their own enrichment with little regard for the needs of others. Some even say they have committed serious crimes. But is there,

---

[152] Which probably demonstrates a lack of interest in following celebrities more than anything else.
[153] Obviously this writer is way out of touch.
[154] See: https://en.wikipedia.org/wiki/Klaus_Schwab.

in fact, any persuasive evidence that at least some members of the Global Elite are guilty of the allegations made against them?

This writer believes that the answer to that question is "yes", particularly in the case of the 9/11 event, the mRNA "vaccine" rollout, and, possibly, private influence on the CIA, and other US government agency, policies. That evidence includes:

Firstly, in the case of the 9/11 event, this writer believes that the case for "insider" involvement in that particular crime has been well demonstrated by two court cases filed in US Courts in 2018 and 2019.[155] Both cases were dismissed on technicalities, their appeals denied and plaintiffs' petitions to the US Supreme Court to review these lower court decisions were also denied. But the evidence itself has never been tested in a court of law nor has it been persuasively rebuked elsewhere. Moreover, this writer finds that evidence overwhelming, irrefutable, without doubt or, to use the legal term, dispositive. This writer believes that if readers were to review the exhibits lodged with US courts in these two cases they would become similarly convinced.

Publication of the document entitled *Rebuilding America's Defenses: Strategy, Forces and Resources for a New Century*[156], by a think tank called *The Project for a New American Century* (PNAC),

---

[155] See petitions filed in 2018 and 2019 by the Lawyers' Committee for 9/11 Inquiry Inc. et al to the U.S. Attorney for the Southern District of New York, case number 1:19-cv-08312-PGC, presenting evidence that explosives were used to take down three buildings in New York City on 9/11/2001 and requesting that a grand jury be convened to consider this evidence. Also see Lawyers Committee for 9/11 Inquiry Inc. et al petition filed in the District Court for the District of Columbia, case 1-19-cv-00824-TNM filed 03/25/19 Document 1, against the United States Department of Justice and the Federal Bureau of Investigation for failing to comply with a 2014 federal law requiring the FBI, and 2014-15 9/11 Review Commission, to review and evaluate evidence not available to it at the time of the 9/11 Commission's inquiry and to report such evidence to congress.

[156] *Ibid*; The Project for the New American Century; Washington, D.C.; September 2000.

suggests to many commentators, that the 9/11 event was pre-planned by an influential group who had previously transited the revolving door between senior government positions and senior private sector appointments. That cohort included Paul Wolfowitz, who later became the Deputy Secretary of State in the George W. Bush administration. The PNAC document famously notes that, to maintain US global dominance would require a significant transformation from its then perceived parlous situation and that: "the process of transformation, even if it brings revolutionary change, is likely to be a long one, absent some catastrophic and catalyzing event – like a new Pearl Harbor[157]."

Neither Paul Wolfowitz, nor any other of his so-called "neoconservative" colleagues, such as then US Vice President Dick Chaney and Secretary of Defense Donald Rumsfeld, could be considered to be members of the Global Elite. But they may have ranked amongst the list of influential people of their time, and they may, in turn, have been influenced by members of the Global Elite. Even the Bush family, with a reported net worth of around US$500 million, would not have made the Forbes billionaire list[158]. One billionaire known to be associated with the 9/11 event is New York businessman Larry Silverstein, reputed to be worth US$5 billion.[159]

Secondly, in the case of the anti-mRNA "vaccine" rollout, there are authoritative voices supporting the allegations of the mismanagement of the global response to the "pandemic".

Evidence of the danger of the Pfizer "vaccine" is presented

---

[157] *Ibid*, p51.
[158] See: https://caknowledge.com/the-bush-family-net-worth/#:~:text=The%20Bush%20Family%20Net%20worth%20The%20world%E2%80%99s%20best,combined%20Net%20worth%20of%20half%20a%20billion%20dollars
[159] See: https://www.wealthypersons.com/larry-silverstein-net-worth-2020-2021/

in an internal Pfizer report obtained via a Freedom of Information request[160]. The Pfizer report shows that 1,223 deaths resulted between 27th December 2020 and 21st February 2021 from 42,806 reported "Adverse Events (AEs)".[161]

But the report itself is of limited use because the total number of Pfizer administered doses of the "vaccine" over that period has been redacted. So, the fatality rate per million doses cannot be calculated and compared to the reported COVID-19 case and death statistics.

However, one might speculate as to what that redacted statistic might be from other data presented in that same Pfizer report. In particular, a graphic on the next page shows that the first two months of the vaccine rollout in the EU was almost exclusively the Pfizer vaccine[162]:

A squint-eye view of the graphic suggests that the number of EU doses administered over that period was about 20 million doses. The report listed the AEs of seven countries[163], with the remaining AEs lumped together within the total for 56 other countries in the full data set.[164]

---

[160] See: https://www.globalresearch.ca/the-pfizer-big-money-maker-have-a-look-at-their-report/5807009.

[161] *Op cit.* and also quoting: "Most cases (34,762) were received from United States (13,739), United Kingdom (13,404) Italy (2,578), Germany (1913), France (1506), Portugal (866) and Spain (756); the remaining 7,324 were distributed among 56 other countries.

[162] The EU rollout on 21st December 2020 trailed the UK rollout on 2nd December 2020 and the US rollout on 11th December 2020.

[163] Those countries were USA (13,739), UK (13704), Italy (2,578) Germany (1,913), France (1,506), Portugal (866) and Spain (756).

[164] At 7,324 Adverse Events (AEs); *Op cit.*: in the preceding note.

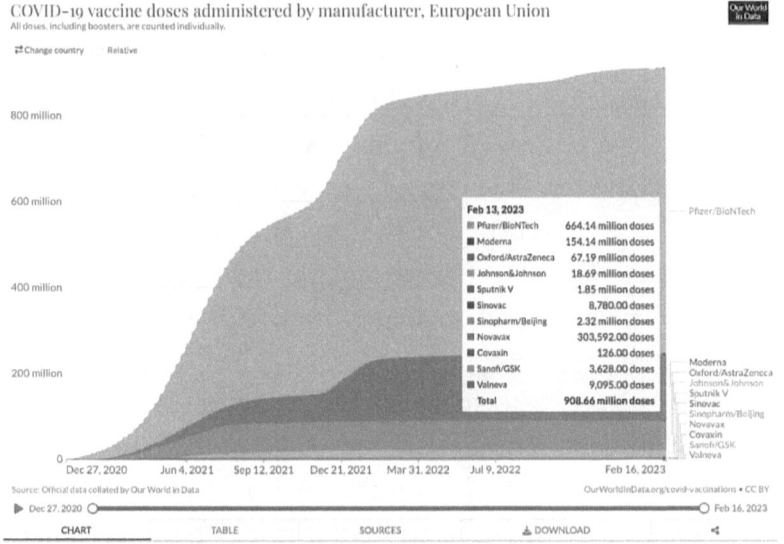

With a few assumptions, the number of total Pfizer doses administered in the subject 8-week period (the redacted statistic) could be estimated at around 72 million doses.[165]

---

[165] If one were to assume that the unlisted countries all had the same approximate average number of AEs, then the unlisted EU countries had around 2,877 AEs between them (i.e. 22/56 of 7,324). That, when added to the known AEs for the five EU countries listed, would give a total number of AEs for the EU as a whole over that 8-week period as 10,496.

Since the US plus UK combined AEs total in the Pfizer report is 27,443 compared to the EU estimate at 10,496 AEs, 2.6 times the then EU total, then the 20 million doses estimated for the EU, could be grossed up 2.6 times to produce an estimate for the US and UK combined at around 52 million doses. Adding this to the 20 million known EU doses gives 72 million doses for the US, UK and EU combined.

How reliable is that estimate?

The Wikipedia reports:

> "The company [Pfizer]...in the last week of July 2020...was slated to be paid $1.95 billion for 100 million doses of the vaccine by the US government" and "in September 2020, Pfizer and BioNTech announced that they had completed talks with the European Commission to provide an initial 200 million vaccine doses to the EU."[166] Given the shape of the curve in the above graphic, which could be assumed to be similar for the US and UK, the above 72 million dose estimate in the first eight weeks of rollout does not seem to be unreasonable.
>
> 1,223 fatalities from 72 million doses would be a "vaccine" fatality rate of around 17 deaths per million doses. This estimate should be compared to the 38 deaths from Guillain Barrée Syndrome that occurred with a Swine Flu vaccine in 1976, given to 45 million people, a dose fatality rate of less than one death per million, which triggered the FDA to declare the injection as having an "unacceptable safety profile".

Clearly the Pfizer "vaccine" is far more lethal than any previously administered vaccine. Good summaries of how lethal were presented at Stockholm's Läkaruppropet (the Doctors' Petition) conference on 21st and 22nd of January 2023, particularly the presentations by Prof Arne Burkhardt, Dr Pierre Kory, Dr Jessica Rose, Dr Richard Urso and Dr Alexandra

---

[166] See: https://en.wikipedia.org/wiki/Pfizer

Latypova.[167]

Data from COVID-19 deaths from the *Worldometer*, as at 22nd February 2023, shows total deaths to that date of 6,792,696 from 678,954,049 recorded cases, a fatality rate of around 1% of recorded cases, or about 10,000 deaths per million cases.[168] Total cases show that just 8.33% of the total world population (i.e. 678.954 million cases /8,147.7 million people) has been infected with COVID-19 to date. This suggests that if COVID-19 had been allowed to run its course, without any intervention, if everyone in the world was to catch it, and if 1% of them actually died from it, then the global fatality rate for COVID-19 would have been over 80 million deaths.

If everyone in the world was vaccinated, at the "vaccine" fatality rate of 17 deaths per million, the resulting projected vaccination deaths would total 138,511 deaths (i.e., 8147.7 million people times 17 deaths per million doses, at one dose only, and twice that much for two doses, on average, at 277,022 projected vaccination deaths). Comparing this to the projected fatalities of 10,000 deaths per million, for those who caught COVID-19, resulting in over 80 million projected COVID-19 deaths, if everyone caught the virus, shows that NOT getting "vaccinated" would have increased your risk of dying from a COVID-19 related event by at least an order of magnitude.

---

[167] See: https://rumble.com/v290q9s-histopathological-reevaluation-serious-adverse-events-and-deaths-following-.html?utm_source=substack&utm_medium=email, https://rumble.com/v2957ew-propaganda-and-censorship-of-effective-generic-drugs-and-the-physicians-who.html?utm_source=substack&utm_medium=email, https://rumble.com/v29r5r4-mrna-technology-lessons-and-consequences-full.html?utm_source=substack&utm_medium=email, https://rumble.com/v29capg-lnpmrna-why-the-covid-jab-is-a-natural-born-killer-full.html?utm_source=substack&utm_medium=email and https://rumble.com/v288sjf-covid-19-countermeasures-evidence-for-an-intent-to-harm-full.html.

[168] See: https://www.worldometers.info/coronavirus/

Of course, the world would never have tolerated such an outcome. In the absence of an effective vaccine, or any other viable treatment, World leaders would have introduced remedial actions to mitigate such a tragedy such as isolating people, mandating face masks, border closures, limited meetings, cancellation of large public events, etc., which is exactly what governments did during the "pandemic", hence the infection of just 8.33% of the world's population.

Some commentators claim that COVID-19 deaths have been overstated. One claimed that only 30% of COVID-19 reported deaths were due to the virus when the deaths were actually due to other causes, cases of people dying "with" Covid-19 not "from" COVID-19.[169] Even if this "real" case fatality rate is accurate, and for the whole world, not just the United States, as this commentator was referring to, then actual COVID-19 deaths worldwide would still be over two million people to date, at a rate of 0.3% of recorded cases, and 14 times the "vaccine" fatality rate.

The above analysis assumes, of course, that there was no other viable treatment for the virus other than a vaccine, which is what the pharmaceutical companies, and all countries mandating vaccination claimed, and which Authorized Emergency Use from the FDA in the US legally required.

But critics of the COVID-19 "vaccine" rollout dispute this. They claim that at least two viable, readily available and safe treatments were available which had been used safely for decades. They were Hydroxychloroquine and Ivermectin. Details of these available alternatives were given by authoritative commentators at the Stockholm conference referred to

---

[169] See: https://nypost.com/2023/01/14/dr-leana-wen-writes-that-covid-deaths-are-being-overcounted/.

above[170].

One example of a state that did embrace the Ivermectin treatment was the Indian state of Uttar Pradesh. Of that state, Dr Pierre Kory has noted:

> "The north Indian state of 241 million people eradicated Covid with an Ivermectin treatment program, representing one of the greatest public health achievements in history. It was kept a global secret."

He reinforces the point with this slide:

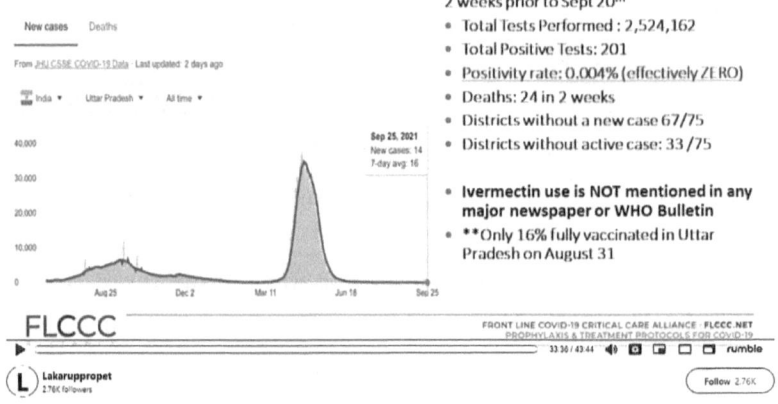

[171]. Others have opined similarly.[172] Others disagree.[173]

Participating governments who mandated the administration of vaccines banned the use of these two treatments on the advice

---

[170] See previous endnote but one and https://lakaruppropet.se/international-conference-pandemic-strategies/.

[171] See: https://expose-news.com/2022/08/13/the-miracle-not-heard-around-the-world/.

[172] See: https://lifestyle.inquirer.net/389302/uttar-pradesh-is-ivermectins-best-practice-success-story/.

[173] See: https://gidmk.medium.com/ivermectin-didnt-save-uttar-pradesh-from-covid-19-17684f49d8b3.

of the World Health Organization. In some cases, they even revoked the medical licences of medical practitioners who prescribed them. In respect of the USA, one scientific journal notes:

"Medical experts that have questioned the safety of these vaccines have been attacked and demonised, called conspiracy theorists and have been threatened to be de-registered if they go against the narrative. Alternative treatments were prohibited and people who never practised medicine are telling experienced doctors how to do their job."[174]

It might be noted that the Bill and Belinda Gates foundation is the second largest donor to the World Health Organization (WHO), second only to the US Government, and that Mr Gates is rumoured to have invested heavily in the pharmaceutical industry since reducing his holdings in Microsoft.

Another source that purports to demonstrate wrong-doing in respect of lethal viruses is a video clip made available by Project Veritas.[175] It purports to show the Director of Research and Development for Pfizer explaining its research into corona viruses which he refers to as "Directed Evolution".

The debate amongst virologists, epidemiologist and medical practitioners is ongoing in respect of the alleged lethality, source, and treatment of COVID-19. Some commentators, including well credentialed academic researchers, allege that mRNA vaccines are toxic.[176]

---

[174] Conny Turni and Astrid Lefringhausen; (2022); *COVID-19 vaccines – An Australian Review*; Journal of Clinical & Experimental Immunology, 2022, 7(3); pp491-508.

[175] See: https://twitter.com/Project_Veritas/status/1618405890612420609.

[176] See: Conny Turni and Astrid Lefringhausen; *COVID-19 vaccines – An Australian Review*; Journal of Clinical & Experimental Immunology; 7(3):491-508; 2002, https://www.globalresearch.ca/age-stratified-covid-19-vaccine-dose-fatality-rate-for-israel-and-australia/5808019 and https://iceni.substack.com/p/psa-why-you-shouldnt-take-the-vaccine#details.

One Australian scientist reports:

"Based on the global number of COVID-19 vaccine doses administered to date (13.25 billion doses, up to 24 January 2023, *Our World in Data*) ... this [i.e. "vaccine" deaths] would correspond to 13 million deaths from the COVID-19 vaccines worldwide. By comparison, the official World Health Organization (WHO) number of COVID-19 deaths to date is 6.8 million (6,817,478 deaths, reported to WHO, as 3 February 2023) ... which are not detected as COVID-19 assignable deaths in [our] ACM [All Causes Mortality] studies."[177]

Meanwhile, governments still recommend getting "vaccinated" and receiving "booster" shots.[178]

This leaves lay observers and the general public confused, whilst pharmaceutical companies have made billions selling "vaccines" to compliant governments.

Thirdly, inappropriate influence by private citizens has been alleged with respect to the direction of the Central Intelligence Agency (CIA) and other US government agencies. Certainly, large campaign donations by wealthy individuals are a well-recognized feature of American politics, particularly by the Political Action Committees (PACs). The activities of the American Israeli Public Affairs Committee, AIPAC, sometimes referred to as Jewish Lobby, and its influence on US Foreign Policy, is also well known and documented by leading political scientists.[179] The revolving door phenomenon between government service and the private sector is a well-known feature of American politics as well. The example of Vice

---

[177] See: https://www.globalresearch.ca/age-stratified-covid-19-vaccine-dose-fatality-rate-for-israel-and-australia/5808019.

[178] See: https://www.health.gov.au/resources/publications/review-of-covid-19-vaccine-and-treatment-purchasing-and-procurement?language=en for an Australian example.

[179] See, for example Mearsheimer, John and Walt, Stephen; *The Israel Lobby and US Foreign Policy*; Farrar, Straus and Giroux; New York; 2008.

President Dick Chaney and his stint as Chief Executive Officer of Halliburton is a case in point. Lucrative private defence industry appointments for retiring senior US military officers are also an alleged well-known influence on US defence spending.

The influence of global funds management guru, billionaire George Soros, reputed to be worth US$10 billion, could be another relevant example. One commentator notes:

> *"Soros has been involved in every Color Revolution since the 1980s including in Yugoslavia, Ukraine, Yeltsin's 1990's rape of Russia, in Iran, against Orbán's Hungary, and countless other countries not playing by the free market 'democracy' agenda of Washington. That is a matter of open record".*[180]

He also notes with respect to India's largest company, Reliance Industries Ltd:

> *"Chairman of Reliance, Mukesh Ambani, is on the Board of the Davos World Economic Forum which is a major promoter of ending crude oil and gas for the UN 2030 Green Agenda.... Ideology is nice but huge profits apparently nicer."*[181]

Fourthly, that some members of the Global Elite occasionally meet, discuss contemporary issues, propose remedies and pass resolutions is well known. Some of the more prominent fora are the Bilderberg Group, the Trilateral Commission, the World Economic Forum and, in times past, the Business Roundtable. But it is not unusual for people of like interests to meet and discuss commonly perceived problems. Unions do it. Environmental groups do it. Church

---

[180] https://www.globalresearch.ca/washington-out-topple-india-modi/5809241.

[181] *Ibid*

denominations do it. Sporting groups do it. It's not illegal. It's not sinister. It's merely the pursuit of self-interest. Anyone can do it. So, it is hardly a crime that needs to be punished.

Fifthly, do leading philanthropists have ulterior motives in their largess? Who knows? Why do people choose to give their money away? Perhaps they feel guilty about past misdeeds known only to the; perhaps they feel embarrassed about their success; perhaps they genuinely care, or perhaps they really do have ulterior motives. Their real motives are known only to themselves. And they are hardly evidence of criminal behaviour.

If the general populous feels that wealthy people are not being generous enough, there are remedies in most countries to address that. One common method is progressive taxation. Another is inheritance taxes or estate duties. Another, less coercive, method is tax deductibility for charitable donations. Many countries have these mechanisms already in place. And as for the hiding of wealth in offshore tax havens and the other legal structures, concerted collaborative efforts by national governments are the remedy to those practices.

These matters are political questions. In democracies, it is the people who should resolve them, via the ballot box.

Has the case of wrong doing been proved?

That nefarious deeds have been done in the past, even the recent past, has been demonstrated, in a few cases, above. That there are unindicted persons who are still at large, and who have committed serious crimes, has also been demonstrated, particularly in the case of the 9/11 event. But even in that case, no specific allegations have been levelled against any specific individuals, although the lawyers for the plaintiffs in the two cases cited have submitted a list of persons whom they believe may be able to give "material evidence" to the US courts. But that list has not been made public. And since both cases have now been dismissed, the American judicial system has seen no need to follow up on that evidence.

It should be noted that, with respect to the 9/11 event, in his review of the 9/11 Toronto Hearings,[182] Mr Justice Ferdinando Imposimato, at that time honorary president of the Supreme Court of Italy, said:

> 'The only possibility to have justice is to submit the best evidence concerning the involvement in 9/11 of **specific individuals**[183] to the ICC[184] Prosecutor and ask him to investigate according the articles…of the Statute of the ICC.'[185]

To the best of this writer's knowledge, this has not yet been done in respect of 9/11. Why not? Perhaps it is because the United States does not recognize the ICC or perhaps because that country has publicly said that it would not tolerate any of its citizens being brought before that judicial body.[186]

Eminent public advocacy lawyer Daniel Sheehan advised similarly in his address to the "Justice in Focus 9/11" conference in New York City in 2016 and in a more recent webinar on the 20th anniversary of 9/11.

With respect to the mRNA 'vaccine' rollouts, the evidence of wrongdoing by some pharmaceutical companies, and perhaps by some public officials, is implied at this time but is circumstantial, and, again, no one has yet been indicted either in the US, the EU or anywhere else that this writer is aware of.

---

[182] See Gourley, James, Ed.; *The 9/11 Toronto Report*, International Hearings on the Events of September 11, 2001; International Centre for 9/11 Studies, Lexington, KY, USA; 2012.
[183] This writer's bolding in emphasis.
[184] International Criminal Court
[185] at pp384-5.
[186] Colloquially referred to as the United States' "Bomb Brussels" policy.

To this writer's knowledge, no specific charges have been brought against specific members of the Global Elite, in any other international forum, for any of the other crimes that have been alleged against them.

With a few possible exceptions, as noted above, it appears that the greatest crime of the Global Elite, as a general class, has merely been its pursuit of self-interest. From the evidence presented, it appears that the political influence of wealthy individuals over public policy, as alleged, is probably indirect, and via various intermediary organizations, rather than by direct control.

What is needed, then, is for accusers to present real verifiable evidence that each accused has actually committed a crime. Moreover, the individual accused should be specifically named and the crime specifically described. And evidence that the accused at least has a case to answer should also be presented when the accusation is made.

A court of law would demand nothing less."

Appendix 8 – Royal Commission's replies in full

On 15th March 2023, I received the following reply to my email of 7th March 2023:

> "Good afternoon, David,
>
> Thank you for providing your feedback, expressing your dissatisfaction with the limited representation of your submission, in our interim report. The Royal Commission is dedicated to providing a transparent and supportive service, and we regret that this has not been your experience.
>
> I recognise your years of dedication, both from your time with the national service and the emergency reserve and acknowledge your veteran status under the definition set by the Royal Commission. Thank you for your service.
>
> The Royal Commission into Defence and Veteran Suicide has be[en] established under the letters patent, to investigate the issues relating to suicide and suicidal behaviours in the Australian Defence and veteran communities, within the scope of our Terms of Reference. The Terms of Reference cover issues like transition, recruitment, ADF culture and the experience of families amongst other themes. The Commission is inquiring into systemic issues, contributing risk factors, as well as protective and

rehabilitative factors that may or may not relate to Defence and veteran suicide.

The Commissioners recognise the importance of hearing from those with lived experience, and have so far received more than 3200 submissions. These submissions are carefully considered by many teams across the Royal Commission, including solicitors, counsellors, policy staff and Counsel Assisting and inform the Commissioners to make meaningful recommendations for change. Submissions published in the Interim Report were identified as being related to the recommendations being proposed in that report. A submission which has not been published at this stage of the Royal Commission may be published at a later date.

We acknowledge that the scope of the task we are undertaking, means we cannot address all issues and concerns bought to us by members of the community, and that this may cause feelings of disappointment.

There is counselling available through the Royal Commission, for those who feel their wellbeing has been impacted by engaging with us. Let me know if you would like me to arrange a call for you.

Please don't hesitate to reach out, should you have any questions, or require support."

On 28th March 2023, I received the following reply to my email of 24th March 2023:

> "Good morning, David,
>
> Once again thank you for alerting the Commission to your concerns about your submission being misrepresented in our Interim Report. We are aware now, that you were wishing to bring to the attention of the Commission your concerns about the Australian Government's engagement in international conflicts and the catalysts for use of Australian Defence Force (ADF) personnel, as opposed to the culture within the ADF, which is an important focus of the Royal Commission.
>
> I would like to offer my assurances that your submission will not be referenced in any future Royal Commission product or content in the context of culture and systems within the Australian Defence Force. We will also update the page that links to our Interim Report on our website with a corrigendum.
>
> I would also like to thank you for sharing your ideas with the Commission. It is only through hearing people's stories and better understanding their experience and insights, that the Commission will be able to make findings and recommendations to help reduce defence and veteran suicides in the future.
>
> While the Commission's inquiries are focussed on issues impacting serving and ex-serving personnel and their families, we appreciate you taking the time to make a submission.
>
> You are welcome to make further submissions as they relate to the Australian Defence Force, this can be done

via the portal on our website here: Make a submission - The Royal Commission into Defence and Veteran Suicide - Citizen Space

The Royal Commission offers counselling services to everyone we engage with, as we know that sometimes the themes we look at can be difficult for people. Please don't hesitate to reach out if you have any questions, or require any further assistance from the Royal Commission."

On 21st April 2023, I received the following reply to my email of 24th April 2023:

"Good morning, David,

Thank you for your email and for your interest in our newsletter, and in the changes to protections being made available to those engaging with the Royal Commission.

The information provided in our newsletter 16 relates to protections available for those sharing confidential information with the Royal Commission. The protections do not relate to communications made by the Royal Commission.

To access legal advice regarding engagement with the Royal Commission, we would encourage you to reach out to the Defence and Veterans Legal Service (DAVLS). DAVLS is a free national service that provides independent information and legal advice to support Australian Defence Force personnel and veterans, as well as their families, carers and supporters, to safely share their experiences with the Royal Commission into Defence and Veteran Suicide.

You are able to contact DAVLS directly on 1800 33 1800 or by email at:

defencevetslegal@legalaid.qld.gov.au.

Please let me know if you have any further questions.

Kind Regards"

Appendix 9 - My AUKUS Submission

Submission to the Australian Parliament regarding the Defence Legislation Amendment (Naval Nuclear Propulsion) Bill 2023

A. For Australia to have an independent, non-aligned defence policy, it would need to have:

1. Dominance of the Timor, Arafura and Coral Seas.

2. Sea denial capability over the chokepoints through the Indonesia archipelago.

3. Sea denial capability over the sea lanes through the Bismarck Sea and Solomon Sea.

4. Cordial and cooperative relations with Indonesia, East Timor, Papua New Guinea, Solomon Islands, New Caledonia (France), Vanuatu, Fiji and New Zealand.

5. Sufficient supplies and ordinance to sustain operations for several months, three to six, without replenishment.

6. A domestic industrial base to supply, service and sustain the forces defending those theatres without replenishment for year-long timeframes.

7. Patrol assets with sufficient range and power to influence events anywhere within the Heard and McDonald

Islands, Cocas/Keeling Island, Christmas Island, Singapore, Manus Island, Norfolk Island, Lord Howe Island, Stuart Island and Macquarie Island perimeters – an operational range of at least 5,000 kilometres [i.e. 5,000 kilometres out and 5,000 kilometres back from their Australian home base port].

8. Disaster relief assets to service emergencies throughout the Indonesian archipelago and Pacific Island Forum states to maintain good neighbour relations.

This would require:

a. Maritime surface patrol capabilities with a range of at least [at least]10,000 kilometres.

b. Maritime strike capabilities against capital ships of carrier battle group size and transport vessels capable of transporting division-sized ground forces with an operational range of 3,000 kilometres [i.e. 3,000 kilometres out and 3,000 kilometres back]:

  i. Surface ships, and

  ii. Subsurface platforms: manned and unmanned.

c. Air Strike assets, both manned and unmanned, with an operational range of 3,000 kilometres [i.e., 3,000 kilometres out and 3,000 kilometres back].

d. Highly mobile ground defence assets deployable to:

  i. Kimberly region of W.A.,

  ii. Coastal Northern Territory, and

iii. Cape York and North Queensland

with deployable range of at least 3,000 kilometres [from their main base].

e. Amphibious transport capabilities for brigade-sized army units with operational range of 3,000 kilometres [i.e. 3,000 kilometres out and 3,000 kilometres back].

f. Long range ground transport vehicles to transport, supply and sustain a division-sized army unit in Northern Australia capable of deploying from Broome to Rockhampton with a range of 3,000 kilometres from their home base.

g. An army of at least one full-time division comprising three joint-arms brigade-sized taskforces, and two reserve divisions.

h. Air defence assets to protect all major capital cities, major northern population centres and military installations with a range of 500 kilometres.

No where in this suite of capabilities does a sub-surface strike capability with a stealth range of 12,000 kilometres seem to be required.

B. Nuclear powered submarines introduce a new highly technical requirement to Australia's naval and defence industry support capabilities that does not currently exist.

C. Australia has difficulty crewing its submarine fleet now. How will it crew boats that require twice the size in crew capacity?

D. Australia will be relying entirely on foreign technical and military knowhow to achieve this capability. How can Australia be assured that this support will be forthcoming from either the United Kingdom and/or the United States ten, twenty and thirty years from now.

E. Even if Australia builds a homegrown capability in this area of expertise, it will be relying on foreign knowhow to build that domestic capability.

F. The United Kingdom's "Global Britain" policy may not endure. It can't really afford that policy now.

G. An American "America First" policy could re-emerge in the foreseeable future. The American people may decide that maintaining the American Empire is not in America's best interests. It happened to the British, French, Dutch, Spanish, Portuguese and Soviet Empires. Why could it not happen to the USA?

H. If military hostilities break out between the United States and China, over Taiwan, or any other issue, the confrontation, and its outcome, are likely to be resolved long before these enhanced capabilities become available. If the outcome is in China's favour, and Australia has backed the United States position, we will have not only alienated our most important trading partner but we will have antagonized Asia's most powerful military and economic power.

I. The nuclear waste from decommissioned submarines will have a long half-life, centuries; it will be toxic long after present generations are gone.

J. Australia could become the dumping ground for the world's nuclear waste, or, at least, that of our allies. In fact, it could become a very lucrative export industry. But how many Australians would support such a proposition? Very few. The only way that could be achieved would be by stealth. Is that what we are seeing with AUKUS?

K. The Force Posture Agreement with United States permits that country to station military equipment, military supplies and ordinance on agreed, designated sites on Australian soil. US policy is to neither confirm nor deny that its military platforms are carrying nuclear weapons and Australia's Foreign Minister has confirmed that the Australian Government respects that policy. In other words: "they don't say and we don't ask". What is to stop the United States military from basing nuclear weapons on those sites without telling us and without us asking?

L. United States has a "nuclear hosting" arrangement with Germany, Italy, Belgium and Netherlands in which those countries "host" US nuclear weapons on their soil, which are under US control, but available for delivery by the armed forces of those countries with US approval. What is to stop the United States entering into a similar arrangement with Australia at some time in the future; especially if we have developed the delivery systems to deliver those weapons?

M. Hosting nuclear weapons would violate the Treaty of Rarotonga. [The second sentence to this bullet point turned out to be wrong in describing its boundary coordinates, and I was obliged to submit a correction two days later, so, that sentence has been redacted here. However, a corrected bullet point might have added: "the Treaty of Rarotonga would not apply to the bases exclusively under the control of a foreign power; as I recently confirmed with my Dutch teleconference interlocutor in the case of the Netherlands, and possibly the other three countries, referred to in L above.]"

About the Author

David Frank Palmer is a former management consultant who specialized in strategic business planning for most of his professional life. His early career was in the banking industry. He later qualified as a Chartered Accountant and commenced private practice in 1982 specializing in financial auditing and tax accounting.

In 1985, he transitioned to the management consulting profession, advising clients on business strategy and marketing strategy. His particular specialty was business planning. That career mostly involved staring at the far horizons trying to anticipate what threats and opportunities were likely to emerge in the decades ahead so as to advise his clients how best to position their organizations to take advantage of the contemporary trends emerging in their markets of interest.

He formally retired in June 2003 from whence he embarked upon a career of formal study and private research. He started writing and publishing in 2009.

Apart from his writing, which has been described in the afore-mentioned narrative, and which has dominated his life since his formal retirement, he has travelled quite extensively, to over fifty different countries across five continents.

He has tutored and lectured part-time at both undergraduate and post-graduate levels at four Western Australian universities in Auditing, Accounting, Financial Management, Marketing, Strategic Management and Management Consulting.

He is married with three adult children – triplets – and two grand-children and lives in Rockingham, Western Australia.

www.ingramcontent.com/pod-product-compliance
Lightning Source LLC
Chambersburg PA
CBHW030036100526
44590CB00011B/232